I

HE WAS WAITING FOR US, of course—hidden behind a wastebasket or tucked under an armchair. As always, when we opened the door of our apartment, I felt that we were stepping into the woods. There was the same sense of small faces watching and listening behind the stillness.

But we were not in the woods. We were in the heart of Manhattan and we had just come home, late in the evening, from taking our two daughters to the ballet. Now Anne and Alice whirled down the hall, still sparkling from the excitement of being up so late—and being *out* so late (the jeweled streets, the improbable city moon)—and still dancing their own ballet to the remembered music. (When you are eight and ten, Mendelssohn is exactly right.) All in all, a magical evening—and a very urban one.

My husband, with an hour of work still to go before finishing a report he had to turn in the next day, was preoccupied, tense, hurrying toward his coffee and his desk. But at heart Jim is a night creature and doesn't mind late hours as much as I do.

As for me, my feet ached and my head ached, and my one thought was to bundle the others off to their appropriate nooks and then collapse gratefully in bed.

But not yet. Because he was waiting. I could feel it. And he had been waiting with growing impatience ever since he woke up at six and trundled out, blinking, to find himself in an empty house.

He had gone first to eat his supper, which was set out in the usual corner. Come what may, he would always eat first. But then he had begun poking and sniffing about, trying to discover where everyone had gone. He had checked and double-checked all the corners, investigated every wastebasket, opened every closet door, catalogued all the smells along the baseboard, rummaged under every bed.

In the end, he had settled himself in some secret den to wait for his family—and most especially, for me. My evening would not be over until he had claimed his share of it.

Now as I stood at the bureau slowly brushing my hair, I heard a soft rustling under the bed.

So that's where you were, my friend! Making a nest in my new velveteen bedroom slippers, no doubt.

A blackberry nose appeared beneath the edge of the bedspread. Cautiously it tested the air. Then a small, wedge-shaped face peered out. Midnight fur, elegant and soft as sable, with a snowy streak down the nose that seemed to have been painted on with a single delicate brush stroke. Precise little ears folded neatly against the head. And shoe-button eyes—rag-doll eyes—shiny bright but very nearsighted. He could see my general outline and he recognized it as familiar, but it was his sense of smell that would confirm who I really was.

He emerged, paw by paw, still sniffing warily. Then, as the full certainty flooded over him—*She is back! She is here!*—he came skittering toward me across the floor.

"Oh no, you don't!" I said. "I know what you have in mind, but not this time!"

I made a flying leap to the middle of the bed. Too late. I scrambled to safety and inspected my ankle, where a curve of tiny needle marks was already beginning to swell. A fine welcome! Was this any way to treat your friends? Lie in wait for them and then bite them?

There was a labored scuffing on the floor. Then two rows of claws appeared over the edge of the bed and clung desperately. With great effort he heaved his fat little self upright and the black button eyes peered at me— nervous, questioning.

Relenting, I scooped him up—an armful of smooth black-and-white fur, warm and musky.

"I know. We were gone a long time and you got upset. But it's all right now. You can relax. Everybody's home."

With a sigh, he settled himself in my lap and turned slightly so that his underside could be rubbed. Satiny and tight as a drum. . . . (Really, I thought, he is eating much too much these days.) Soon he would be up and dashing about the house, challenging me to a game of tag. But, for the moment, he just sighed again and closed his eyes peacefully.

11

Not such a bad little skunk, after all.

But why did we have a skunk in the first place?

He was no foundling discovered by the roadside, no starving infant huddled close to his dead mother's body. Nor was he saved from the talons of an attacking owl or pried out of a trap.

Such a rescue-plus-adoption would have been romantic. (It would also have been illegal: In most states it is against the law to keep a wild skunk. Some city health departments ban keeping a skunk from any source as a house pet, on the rather odd theory that since wild skunks are sometimes exposed to rabies, all skunks should therefore be prohibited. Just what you are supposed to do if you come upon some lost orphan, I am not sure. Call the state police, no doubt, and let *them* cope.)

No, our skunk came to us from a Minnesota fur farm, by way of a New York pet shop. Whenever unsympathetic friends have disapproved of taking a wild animal out of his natural environment, we have been able to agree with a clear conscience. If this one hadn't found a home with us (or with somebody), he would have been a fur coat.

Which still does not answer the question of why we chose a skunk as a house pet and not, let us say, a goldfish. It is a question I have asked myself many times in the far clear hours of dawn. (Such periods of wakefulness are all too common if you have a nocturnal animal in residence.)

Ten-year-old Alice gave her own reason in a piece she wrote for the fifth-grade newsletter. It is as good as any other.

"We needed a pet," she wrote, "but my father is

12

illergic to cats and my mother did not feel up to a dog just then. So we got a skunk."

We did need a pet, that much was certain. Our girls are the sort of children who really require an animal, just as other children may require extra vitamins or day camp. And for many years they had been making do with the usual assortment of city-apartment pets.

There were the dour little turtles who inevitably went blind and had to be nursed back to health with heat lamps and cod-liver oil. It is quite a trick, incidentally, to get medicine into one of these little creatures. He may be only the size of a quarter, but he is unbelievably stubborn and he does not like having an eye dropper stuck down his gullet. As soon as he senses your approach, he sinks to the bottom of the tank and stays there. You hang over the rim, growing more and more nauseated by the smell of the cod-liver oil, until your victim is finally forced to come up for a gulp of air, at which point you lunge. When, after weeks of treatment, he at last recovers, you give him away to the nearest nursery school.

We had also had the traditional succession of rodents: the testy little guinea pigs, who do nothing but squeal for food and spill water all over their cages; the mice and gerbils, enchanting to hold in your hand but depressing to watch as they rush endlessly about their glass case, trying to climb the slippery walls to freedom; and of course the hamsters, who sleep all day and then whirl insanely on their little exercise wheels all night.

Then there were the tadpoles, who refused to eat anything except crumbs of hard-boiled egg yolk waggled before their noses on a toothpick. And the baby frogs, who required a never-ending feast of flies, preferably live ones. (If dead, the flies had to be whisked about on a broomstraw so that they *seemed* to be alive.) These pets usually wound up in the Central Park lake, transported there by the jarful in my husband's elegant attaché case.

And there was the gentle pastel salamander who did nothing at all except fade slowly into death.

Snakes we never tried.

Among the more satisfactory pets was Tippy, a merry little Dutch rabbit with a handsome black coat and snowy vest. He was far too lively to be kept in his cage, and we had to let him hop about the house. He left pink urine stains in all the corners and crunchy piles of droppings behind the door, but he was so charming that we were prepared to forgive a good deal.

We had had Tippy for only two weeks when he developed a mysterious fever (he had brought it with him from the pet shop, apparently), stopped eating, and died.

And then for one utterly wild week end, we played host to Fluffy, the first grade's pet duckling. However, by the time our turn came to have him as a week-end guest, he was not exactly a duckling any longer—more like a goose. His baby-soft yellow down was almost gone, and he had strange naked patches ringed with scruffy white pinfeathers. He had not yet developed his adult quack, but he talked continuously in a sort of strangled gurgle. And he was clever, strong, and opinionated.

He arrived in an enormous carton which would presumably house him for the week end. In five seconds he had clambered out; looked us over, first with one intelligent, appraising eye and then the other; sized us up (correctly) as easy marks; and set off down the hall with the rolling gait of a pirate, intent on finding water and food.

We herded him back into the pantry and shut the door while we pulled ourselves together. Obviously we could not keep him in that box. Anne knelt down and put her eye to the crack of the pantry door. She found herself staring into Fluffy's eye, which was also right at the crack.

We decided to let him out in the kitchen, hoping that if he got some exercise, he would be willing to settle down. Then we spent the rest of the afternoon mopping the floor with paper towels, since ducks do not seem to notice where they are walking and tramp across their drinking dish, bathroom paper, and food pan with casual disregard, mixing everything into a wet, smelly mess. Also they never seem to stop talking.

Finally we tried putting him into the bathtub. This, we thought, might keep him occupied for a while and quiet that incessant croaking. Fluffy was enchanted. He flicked his stump of a tail and paddled importantly about, pausing occasionally to reach underwater and peck at the chipped marks on the floor of the tub. But when we tiptoed out and shut the door behind us, the result was a bloodcurdling screech.

"He's lonesome," Anne explained. "He thinks he's one of the school children, and he wants people to play with him all the time."

We were only too happy to send this particular child back to school on Monday.

We even had a bird briefly, although it was against our principles. All of us are opposed to the very idea of caged birds, but we found this one—somebody's pet green finch—hunched miserably on the city sidewalk one cold night. My husband carried it home inside his shirt, and we tried desperately to nurse the disconsolate little bundle of feathers back to health. He managed to survive a week or so, but the shock had been too much for him, and soon an empty bird cage joined the empty aquarium, mouse tank, guinea-pig cage, rabbit box, and other containers in our storeroom.

"The trouble with all the pets we've had so far," Alice decided, "is that none of them have been very *rewarding*." She had just finished her vocabulary homework.

"Yes," Anne agreed, "we need a real pet. A kitten, maybe, or a horse, or a puppy."

My own first requirement was for a pet that might have a chance of surviving. We had had enough funerals for a while. I also hoped for one that wouldn't demand my constant attention every waking hour. A new puppy would be like a new baby, I felt, and that particular year I had other projects in mind. A horse was not too practical for a city apartment. My husband's main stipulation was that it must not make his eyes swell shut—hence, no kitten.

Somehow, it seemed very logical to get a skunk.

It was early July when the news came that our pet had finally arrived in New York. We had closed our city apartment for the summer and were just getting settled in the old farmhouse in Connecticut. The first heat wave of the season had also arrived, and we were not exactly enthusiastic about spending the entire day in the car, driving into the city to pick up our new pet and then returning directly to the country. But acquiring a skunk is a seasonal achievement and we had no choice.

Skunks are usually conceived in February or March,

born in April, weaned in May—and sold in June. Ours was not available until July, owing to delays in ordering and shipping which we never fully understood. As a result, he was nine weeks old when he came to the pet shop, though he was still very small: clearly the runt of the litter. The usual age for getting a baby skunk is six weeks, which is the recommended age for taming. We knew that every day our own skunk spent imprisoned and alone would make it that much harder for him to adjust to a different way of life. So when the pet-shop owner telephoned, we were on our way to New York almost immediately.

He was about as big as a chickadee when we first saw him—and about as friendly as a baby wasp.

Most skunks tend to be quite amiable. They do not seem to have any inborn fear or dislike of men. If anything, the opposite is true. A wild skunk will often make his den underneath a barn or a woodshed, establishing an entente cordiale with the family dog and other barnyard residents, and repaying the farmer for his hospitality by keeping the vegetable garden free of caterpillars and field mice.

But our little skunk had, after all, been born on a fur farm, in a world of gravel runs and steel mesh fences. He had been separated from his mother while still a baby and shipped across country in a barred case. Then he had spent three weeks in a city pet shop, hiding under a pile of shredded newspaper in the corner of an old aquarium. Somewhere along the line he had undergone a descenting operation, probably without anesthetic. We should not have been surprised, then, the day we came to get him, to see the pet-shop owner draw on thick leather gauntlets. But we were.

"Is he apt to bite?" we asked apprehensively.

"No, no," the owner assured us, "he just likes to bluff a little."

With a practiced swoop, he grabbed the little skunk by the back of the neck, as if he were capturing a rattlesnake, and dumped him hastily into the grocery carton we had brought. Our new pet scrambled to his feet, whirled in the direction of our voices, flared his tail in the classic warning signal, and then brought his front feet down on the box floor with an astonishingly loud thump. He paused, as if for effect. Then he thumped again.

Later we came to recognize this as his special rhythm. Three beats: one long, two short. THUMP (pause)— thump, thump. Almost a tom-tom rhythm, except that it had only three beats instead of four.

Anne melted. "Oh, the poor little thing," she crooned lovingly. "He must be awfully scared."

Her sister was skeptical. "Do you really think he's scared? To me he looks just plain mad."

"I told you we should have gotten another guinea pig," my husband said.

II

ONCE IN THE CAR for the return trip to Connecticut, the grocery carton rattled and shook with our new pet's determined assaults as he endeavored to scrabble up the sides. The girls held down the top with both hands, although the box was so large that even on tiptoe he could never have reached the rim. At the same time they managed to keep their faces turned toward the car windows, like princesses in a royal limousine, hoping to see some passing school friend who could be beckoned over to the car for the surprise of her life.

Over and over, for a full half-hour, the little skunk kept up his efforts—scratch and fall, scratch and fall.

"He's going to hurt himself!" Anne kept exclaiming. "Can't we do something to make him stop?" She bent close to the box and hummed soothing songs.

Abruptly, there was complete silence. Alice opened the cover a crack and peered inside.

There, in the farthest corner, curled into a tiny ball, was our skunk. He was fast asleep.

Of all the smaller wild animals, the skunk is surely the most sensible. Finding himself caught in some apparently hopeless situation, he does not waste a moment on panic. Rather, he stubbornly sets to work trying to free himself. His determination in the face of repeated frustrations is incredible. He works and works and *works*, testing first one approach and then another. Not for him the frozen resignation of a trapped rabbit, the frantic terror of a squirrel, or the savage desperation of a weasel, which may even rip or bite its way out of a trap, leaving a leg or paw still caught in the iron jaws.

Pragmatism is the skunk's middle name. Once he realizes that no amount of effort, however determined, is going to accomplish anything, he stops trying. He does not brood or grieve or worry. He simply settles himself down as comfortably as possible and calmly goes to sleep.

There is a lesson here, I expect.

So we brought our baby skunk, sleeping soundly, to his new home and to a new life of freedom.

In his case, of course (as in so many cases), freedom would be relative. I certainly did not propose to let him roam at will around the house—not, at any rate, in the beginning. Not until he was house-trained. But this would be only a matter of days. The pet-shop owner had assured us that skunks are the easiest of all animals to house-train. In the meanwhile, he would have to spend part of his time in a cage.

I comforted myself with the reflection that this was no ordinary cage. Occupying almost one-third of the utility room we call the back kitchen, it was a gleaming enclosure of silver bars and mirror-bright floor, raised high on sturdy legs above any possible draft. (So high, in fact, that we had to put a small log in front of the doorway as a step.) It had a grated cover and a splendid portcullis and was strong enough, as my husband remarked, to hold a bobcat.

The cage was furnished with a neat box of cat litter and a huge scarlet drinking bowl which had once belonged to my mother's Irish setter, Holly. Skunks are great drinkers and the usual small water dish would not do. At the back of the cage was an enchanting little house which Alice and Anne had made from a shoe box. Across the top Anne had painted a procession of beaming daisies, while over the door was a sign—SKUNK'S HOUSE—printed in Alice's most elegant curlicues. Inside was a fragrant bedding of cedar chips.

All in all, it was quite a cage. What is more, I had paid an unforgivable $16.98 for it—at the reduced sale price. But at least our new pet would be comfortable. He might even enjoy his new quarters. It's possible to grow quite fond of a cage, provided that it is roomy and comfortable. Such, at least, has been my own experience.

Jim carried the grocery carton into the kitchen and gently set it down next to the cage. Then he opened the cover. The response was instantaneous.

THUMP—thump, thump! No misunderstanding that drum-beat message: Stay away! Don't come any closer. The first one who touches me will be sorry.

Standing almost on tiptoe, his back arched, fur bristling, tail fanned into a plume twice as big as the rest of him, the little skunk glared up at us and drummed again.

For a moment we gazed down helplessly at the furious bit of fluff.

"You know, Mom," said Alice thoughtfully, "this isn't going to be so easy."

"Yes," said Anne, "we may have quite a job here, Mom."

Their father tactfully refrained from comment.

"He just needs a little time to adjust," I said with a cheery confidence that I did not feel. "Let's put him in his cage and leave him alone for a while to settle down. We can go and have something to eat. Then we'll give him his own lunch and start trying to make friends."

"*You* put him in his cage," Alice said promptly.

Anne took one step backward, crossed her arms behind her, and looked small and helpless.

Jim grinned. "Good idea," he said. "After all, getting a skunk was really your idea in the first place. You should be the one to do the honors."

I certainly was not going to try to pick him up with my bare hands. Lacking a capture stick with a noose, or some sort of drawstring net, we would have to dump him out.

"He won't like that," Anne predicted with undoubted accuracy. But it was clearly the only way.

The carton was too large for me to handle alone, but Jim, who had never really intended to abandon the situation, hefted it easily. The girls and I each took a corner, and together we raised it to the top of the cage. Then we tipped it slightly. The little skunk went slipping and sliding down into his new enclosure. He landed almost without sound. Thistledown. Dandelion puff. Shadow.

Then BANG went his front paws on the resounding metal floor. It was like the off-stage thunderclap in a high school play. BANG—bang, bang.

"We'd better leave him alone now," I said, herding the girls away and shutting the back-kitchen door behind us. "Let's have lunch—how about grilled cheese sandwiches or maybe bacon and tomato? Don't worry about the skunk. When we go back, he'll surely be feeling better."

When we went back, he was gone.

It was impossible. The door of the cage was still latched firmly, the top fastened tightly. There did not seem to be any conceivable way that he could have gotten out.

The fact remained that he was gone.

"He couldn't have slipped between the bars!" exclaimed Alice. But it was clear that he must have done exactly that.

"Well, he's got to be here in the back kitchen somewhere," Jim said. "We'll just have to organize a systematic search. Each person take one-quarter of the area."

So we did. Creeping about on hands and knees, occasionally bumping into one another, we proceeded to hunt for our missing pet.

There were plenty of good hiding places in the old summer kitchen: inside the broom closet (which has no door), under the ancient radiator, beneath the cupboards that line two of the walls, and behind the woodpile (for reasons too complicated to explain, there happened to be a pile of apple logs in one corner, waiting to be transferred to the woodshed).

We found quite a few things: an old tennis ball, Anne's missing sneaker, a dead moth, a fine chunk of mica, part of a candy cane (a candy cane? in July?), a green doll comb, seven house spiders (not all in one corner), and what appeared to be a fossilized peach-stone. But no skunk.

"There's only one place we haven't checked," Anne said, sighing. "The washing machine. And it would be simply impossible for him to squeeze under there."

The square, bulky front-loader has a space of an inch and a half or perhaps two inches underneath, not more.

"I'm beginning to think nothing is impossible for this animal," Jim said as he reached for a flashlight. Stretching flat on the floor, he shone the beam under the washer, and we all flopped down to join him.

"Good grief!" Alice whispered. "Will you look at that?"

We were staring into the face of a very small, very irate field mouse.

For over a year, the occasional cats who came to visit us had been insisting that Someone Lived Under There. But I had not paid much attention, since there were no other signs—no telltale crumbs, no nibbled cereal boxes, no tiny droppings like black seeds on the kitchen counter. He had been a perfect tenant, sleeping here but dining elsewhere.

Now the state of peaceful coexistence had been disrupted. Upset but determined, he faced the intruders, his whiskers quivering in outrage.

"Oh, Mom!" Anne breathed. "Can we keep him? Just imagine having a field mouse for a pet!"

At the moment I was more concerned with having a skunk for a pet.

Jim turned the light away from the field mouse and swept the beam from side to side. Then he held it steady.

"Look there," he said.

In the farthest, darkest, dustiest corner, we saw a ball of black-and-white fur. Sleeping, of course.

It was a pretty good den for a small animal, all things considered. Not as nice as a mossy crevice under a ledge of granite, perhaps, but dark and cozy and undeniably safe. What is more, it probably had a comforting outdoors smell, thanks to having a mouse nest in the nearby baseboard. The little skunk's instinct had served him well.

If we had known more about skunks, we would have looked under the washing machine at the very beginning. Nowadays, whenever I walk into a strange room, I find myself automatically surveying it for possible skunk dens.

My expertise in this matter was confirmed last spring when our entire family—skunk included—went to visit cousins who had just moved into a new house in Princeton, New Jersey. I was sitting in the kitchen having coffee with our hostess when the children trooped in shouting, "We can't find the skunk! We've lost the skunk!"

"Look in the living room," I suggested, "under the big green armchair." I had spotted that chair as soon as I walked into the house. A moment later, a whoop of joy from the next room told me I was right.

Living with a wild animal certainly gives you a new perspective.

But that first afternoon as we crouched in front of the washing machine, we had to consider a new problem.

Finding our skunk in his improvised den was one thing; extricating him was quite another.

"Maybe we could sort of nudge him out," Alice suggested. We soon discovered, however, that our yardstick was missing, and the mop handle would not go all the way under. So we had to give up the idea of gently poking our reluctant pet into the open.

Jim brought the emergency flashlight from the car, hoping to dazzle him awake. But a skunk sleeps with his head tucked underneath and wouldn't notice a theatrical spotlight centered right on him. My own suggestion was to turn on the washing machine. It is one of the earliest models of the front-loading type, an asthmatic monster whose wheezings and clangings can be heard all the way to the front gate. It drives *me* out of the kitchen entirely and as far away as possible—in fact, to the opposite side of the house.

We tried it. Soon a Niagara of hot water was pouring into the metal drum directly over the small sleeper's head, while the motor was starting up its unbelievable clangor all around him.

As his audience, prone on the kitchen floor, watched breathlessly, the ball of fur moved slightly. Then one shiny eye blinked at us.

I concentrated hard. Look, little one—there's nothing to be afraid of. Be a good skunk now and come out.

He appeared to consider his situation, listening to the uproar above him and weighing the possible dangers in the open kitchen. Then he made up his mind. He settled himself more snugly in his corner, tucked his head out of sight, and went back to sleep.

"Might as well give up," Jim said. "He's bound to get

hungry sooner or later and then he'll come out of his own accord."

"When will that be?" Anne wanted to know.

"Certainly by evening," I said. "And maybe sooner."

III

Dusk came at last—the gauzy lavender dusk of early summer—and with it the soft thud of insects against the screen door and the merest feather of a breeze. It was time for a small nocturnal creature to be shaking himself awake. It was moth-time—which for a skunk means suppertime.

But underneath the washing machine, all was silence. Still exhausted from the day's excitement and from the disruption of his inborn time schedule, the new arrival slept on.

As for us, we hovered.

Anne tiptoed in and out of the back kitchen all evening, hoping to surprise him if he emerged. Alice, who has monumental patience, lay on the floor beside the washer for at least half an hour, still as a stone. And when at last the girls reluctantly trailed off to bed, I myself took up the vigil, checking and rechecking the back kitchen at intervals right up until midnight.

Jim, seemingly unconcerned, worked at his desk.

By the time I had finished my shower, I was growing genuinely anxious.

"Do you think he's all right, Jim?" I worried. "Do you think he's still alive under there? Maybe we ought to get the flashlight and see."

"Well, as a matter of fact," my husband admitted, "I already have. I took a look at him while you were in the shower. He seems to be fine. Just tired, that's all. And come to think of it, so am I—aren't you?"

I was. It had been a long day for us all. So I set out fresh water and some of the cat food we'd brought from the pet shop, putting them inside the cage and tying the door open. Perhaps if he learned to associate the cage with meals, he might be more willing to stay in it.

"I only hope that he'll come out sometime during the night," I said.

There was no need to worry: he came out, all right. The next morning, the back kitchen looked as if he had tried to take it apart. It also looked as if he had had ten other little skunks to help him.

The woodpile had been toppled over and logs were scattered all across the floor. A half-filled trash basket lay on its side, the contents shredded into long, neat strips (just right for papier maché, Anne pointed out admiringly) and strewn around the room.

In the cage, the cat-litter pan had been turned upside down and so had the Skunk House. There were mounds of sand and cedar chips everywhere. Instead of the litter pan, each corner of the kitchen floor had been used as a bathroom. Someone had been swimming in the scarlet water dish. The food dish had been polished clean and then pushed out of the cage door and over to the washing machine. (It was too large to go underneath.)

Finally, the cupboard doors had all been tested and the one latch that did not close properly had been discovered. The door was open and the cupboard was bare. Inside it we had been storing a huge gunny sack of birdseed left over from the winter feeding. Now the whole supply spilled out among the apple logs. This must have been the most glorious adventure of all—imagine climbing about on sierras of birdseed!

The back kitchen was, in short, an awesome sight. Meanwhile, the cause of all this chaos was safe in his den under the washing machine, sleeping the sleep of the innocent.

Wading ankle-deep in birdseed, armed with shovels as well as brooms and a mop, we plunged into what was clearly going to be the major project of the morning.

"And to think," said Alice plaintively, "we haven't even had a chance to hold him yet!"

"I haven't even had a chance to get a good look at him yet," Anne mourned.

So far, this new addition to our household was proving to be more of a problem than a pet.

When the back kitchen had finally been restored to some sort of order (although for weeks afterward we would keep stepping on stray grains of birdseed), we adjourned to the pond for a well-earned swim.

Next came a round of sandwich making (a different kind for each member of the family, needless to say) and after that we all dispersed: my husband to drive into New

York for an afternoon meeting, Alice to practice her violin under the old apple tree in the back yard (and incidentally to test whether the birds would respond, which they did not), while I myself went to enjoy a glass of iced tea and—at last!—the morning paper, down by the pond in the little screened summerhouse still known as the Barbecue, although the fireplace which inspired its name fell apart years ago.

Anne could not decide just what she was going to do. What she really wanted was to play with the new pet, but this, of course, was out of the question. She later told us that she lay down on the back-kitchen floor, taking occasional bites of her second bacon and tomato sandwich, and peered hopefully under the washing machine. For a while, she talked softly and encouragingly to the unresponsive ball of fur in the corner. She tried calling, "Here, Stripey." The name didn't sound quite right. "Come here, Midnight—here, Middie!" That one wasn't right either.

At last she gave up and walked over to the screen door to watch her sister—still in a yellow bathing suit, wet hair plastered on her shoulders—playing Vivaldi to the sparrows.

A piece of bacon from the sandwich fell unnoticed to the floor. Unnoticed by Anne, that is.

There was a scratching under the washer and then a jet black nose appeared at the edge, sniffing excitedly. Anne gave what she later described as "only a very tiny squeak" and the nose vanished. But the bacon vanished with it. A moment later the sound of happy crunching came from under the washing machine.

Anne flew to announce the good news. "He came out! He came out!"

"You mean you actually *saw* him?" her sister said sharply. "It's not fair! Last night I waited there for hours!"

I intervened quickly. "Do you have any of that sandwich left, Anne?"

Luckily she did: almost a third of it remained, including a sizable strip of bacon. The girls laid a Hansel and Gretel trail of crumbs and bacon bits all the way from the washing machine to the cage, where they set out the final scraps in a neat row. Then we tiptoed to the farthest side of the kitchen and waited to see if the lure would work.

It did.

Almost at once we heard a scrabbling under the washer, then the inquisitive nose came poking out. A moment later an eager baby skunk was eating his way to the cage. If he noticed that we were there, he did not seem to care. His mind was on other things, chiefly bacon.

As soon as he had clambered up the doorstep log and into the cage, I dashed over to lower the portcullis and lock him inside. It was a futile gesture, of course, since he could escape whenever he pleased simply by slipping through the bars. But I had not yet accepted the fact that such an impressive contraption was, for him, nothing more than a feeding station.

Now he raised his head, a shred of bacon dangling from his mouth, shot a scornful look in our direction, and hammered out his triple-beat warning, complete with peacock tail. He waited a moment to be sure that the message would be respected, then lowered his tail and went back to his eating.

"Quick!" I whispered to the girls. "Now's our chance! We've got to block up that space under the washing machine. Run and get some books!"

While I stood guard over the little skunk, ready to head him off if necessary, the girls flew to the living room. (They never move that fast on school mornings.) They came back laden with everything from Shakespeare to Thurber, and before long the washer displayed under and around its base a sort of terrace, constructed with the help of some of our favorite authors. The final selection was dictated by size rather than relevance, of course, but *Walden* was there, appropriately enough, and *The Call of the Wild,* and *The Cordon Bleu Cook Book* (which a skunk would love if he could read). I tried hard to wedge in *The Territorial Imperative* but it would not fit.

"But what about the field mouse?" Anne worried.

"He must have a special passage inside the wall," I told her as I shoved another volume into place. "Probably leading down to the cellar."

(There are all sorts of chinks in the field-stone walls of the old cellar: the girls are forever finding discarded snakeskins down there, like cellophane ribbons dropped on the dirt floor, and every so often they come upon a stray toad or beetle.)

Reassured that we were not building a mouse prison, the girls quickly helped me finish the task. Not a moment too soon, either. The morsel of Anne's sandwich had just been devoured and now, as the excitement of eating began to fade away, the baby skunk suddenly realized that he was alone, out in the open, in alien territory.

Instantly he scurried to the door of the cage, paused only a second at finding it closed, then simply *flowed* between the bars.

Before we ourselves could move, he had whisked across to the washer, skidded to a stop in front of the unexpected literary barricade, then flashed away to the radiator, and was gone.

Later in the afternoon Jim phoned from New York to say that he would be late for dinner.

"By the way, how's the skunk?" he inquired.

"Oh, the skunk's fine, just fine," I assured him.

"Any luck getting him out from under the washing machine?"

"Well, yes, as a matter of fact."

"Hey, that's quite an achievement! Congratulations! Where is he now?"

"Under the radiator."

IV

WEARILY BUT STUBBORNLY we resumed the battle. The radiator was not so easy to barricade as the washer had been—the open space was larger and complicated with pipes. Still, every evening before we went to bed we lured the little skunk to the far end of the kitchen, trapped him under an overturned carton, and then rushed to block up his new den.

We spent almost an hour arranging our best small fireplace logs to fit tightly into his sleeping space. It took him three minutes to push them out again.

We lugged armloads of stones from the garden (which in true Connecticut fashion produces a better crop of granite than of anything else) and heaved them under the radiator. For good measure, we shoved stones under the cabinets as well and arranged massive piles in all the corners, hoping to prevent their use as bathroom areas. The back kitchen looked like some sort of weird rock garden but never mind.

This was when we learned why a skunk has such long, curving claws. They are not sharp like a cat's, but they are incredibly strong: grizzly-bear claws in miniature. And they are especially designed for uprooting and overturning rocks.

"Let's try suitcases," Jim suggested. "We can load them up with books, so they'll be too heavy for him to push around."

We tried it, even though it added a new complication to any search for a favorite book. ("If it isn't under the washing machine, it might be in the blue suitcase.") The resultant baggage barricade was far too heavy for *me* to move without a good deal of assistance. It posed no problem at all to a homing skunklet no bigger than a pine cone.

Every night we closed the back-kitchen door, hoping that this time we had finally managed to erect a skunk-proof barrier. And every morning we dolefully faced yet another defeat as we bent down to look at the small sleeper tucked safely among the cobwebs.

Jim and the girls were willing to give up long before I was. But in the end, even I agreed that we had to let our skunk have his way. So he made himself a nest of shredded paper (the kitchen trash basket offered an excellent assortment), and there he stayed, under the radiator.

A few weeks later, he grew too big to squeeze into such inconvenient corners. It was a solution I had not foreseen.

Looking back on it now, I ask myself why I was so intransigent. The new nest was not in a bad location: it was fairly accessible and yet out of the main stream of traffic. Why did I make such a major issue out of such a minor matter? After all, as Anne said, what's so bad about having a skunk living under your kitchen radiator?

That first skirmish, and the series of conflicts which followed it, brought out a side of me which I did not recognize. Normally, I am not so rigid in my rules, so stubborn in my expectations. With Alice and Anne I have always been, I think, quite flexible: even—for a parent—quite reasonable (apart from an admittedly irrational prejudice against long bangs). It has never bothered me when the children took their time about any particular stage of development, whether it was learning to use a spoon or graduating from diapers or moving out of the crib. And whenever either girl has developed an odd quirk, I have usually managed a calm acceptance. If someone felt a compulsion to wash her hands all the way to the elbow *three* times before every meal, well, it was all right with me—provided that she made it to the table before her meat loaf got cold.

Moreover, I have lived for years in close relationship with various forms of wildlife and have never felt the need to impose my will on any of them. I resignedly share my back-yard drink with the wasps; post signs around the front door every spring to warn visitors that the same hysterical robin is nesting again in the eaves directly over the door; and remind swimmers to splash the pond before they go in, so that the huge snapping turtle dozing somewhere in the muddy depths can withdraw in peace to the far end.

I detour patiently around the back step whenever the old black snake is sunning himself there, and I do not even object too strongly when the squirrels rob the bird feeder.

After all, how can they be expected to know it's not the birds who are robbing the squirrel feeder?

As for our earlier house pets, my attitude toward their foibles and eccentricities was always tolerant to the point of overpermissiveness. In the past, "Live and let live" had been my motto. But now, faced with a baby skunk who wanted to sleep under the radiator and not in his assigned house, I became a rock of resistance. Why, I cannot say.

Perhaps it was because this was the first time I had tried to integrate a wild creature into our family pattern. Wasps and robins obviously belong to the out of doors—they are not my responsibility—while mice and gerbils are shelf pets, not potential members of the family. And the dogs and cats I remember from my childhood were domesticated to begin with.

Perhaps I was caught in a modern reenactment of an ancient struggle, reaching back to the time when primitive man first began to sort out the wild animals he saw around him and discover which ones could be tamed and which could not. Certainly there was an almost atavistic grimness to my determination. And pride was probably involved as well.

At any rate, something in the little skunk's stubbornness kindled in me an answering stubbornness. He chose one spot as his den; I decreed another. Neither of us was ready to give an inch.

It was a contest of wills which would be repeated in various forms over and over during that first year. Time and again I would make an attempt to train our new pet, as you would train a new puppy or kitten, granting due allowance for individual crotchets ("Our cat simply refuses to eat tuna fish"; "We absolutely cannot break our dachshund of barking at the telephone") but nevertheless insisting that, in most areas, he adapt to his human family.

It took me a long time to accept the fact that, with a skunk, the situation is reversed. You do not train him; he trains you.

A skunk is a wild animal, even though he may have been born in captivity, and he never fully accepts domesticity. Oh, he likes people well enough—may even grow attached to one or two of them—and he certainly likes the comforts of life which they can provide. But he never comes to depend on people, as some other animal might. And, unlike a domestic animal, he never tries to please anyone but himself. It is not a skunk's nature to study your face speculatively, kitten fashion, trying to decide what you are thinking. Nor will he come beaming up to you with the typical puppy present: a lovely dead frog, perhaps, or your best scarf chewed to shreds.

As for expecting a skunk to regulate his sleeping, eating, or excreting habits in order to conform to some human requirement, this is totally out of the question. He is aware of human displeasure—he hates being shouted at and will try to avoid it whenever convenient—but it never enters his head to alter his own behavior even a fraction in order to win human approval. He simply can't be bothered.

No matter what the issue—diet, house-training, daily routine, or whatever—it is the humans who must finally adapt. Life would have been much easier for us all if I had been able to accept the inevitable more gracefully.

The struggle was not exclusively my own, of course. The rest of the family were continually involved. Yet it soon became clear that this stubborn little newcomer, originally intended as a pet for Alice and Anne, was in fact mine. (Or as much mine as anybody's.) Mine by default. I was around when he was; the others were not.

We could have altered his nocturnal pattern, but such an undertaking requires sustained effort. And on a summer day, there are so many other things to do. It is temptingly easy to let sleeping skunks lie while you yourself go for a picnic to Roxbury Brook.

So it turned out that, as a rule, the skunk was feeling most active just when the girls were brushing their hair for bed and Jim was settling down at his desk—which left me alone on the field of battle. And if in the end I seldom gained a clear cut victory, I did gain a special insight into my small adversary's mind and an admiration for his tenacity.

V

SMALL GOBBLER OF BEETLES AND POTATO CHIPS, cricket cruncher, connoisseur of caterpillars and casseroles—what struggles we used to have at every mealtime!

"Cat food," I would insist. "Cat food seasoned with vitamin powder."

"Table scraps," would come the response. "Hot rolls and roast beef and *seedless* grapes."

Also pizza, chocolate ice cream (never vanilla), and fried shrimp.

Salad greens, but only if accompanied by a good vinegar and oil dressing.

Buttered toast, of course—first to be used as a skateboard when nobody is looking and later to be munched in bed.

Apples and bananas if cut in neat wedges.

Cheddar cheese in any form.

But above all, the prime favorite: bacon. (Very crisp, of course.)

Bait, bribe, reward, and prize—a bit of bacon is all of these and more. When a pet skunk, shut in the pantry of a city apartment for the night, awakens the whole family at 2:30 A.M. with his persistent scratching, a bit of bacon slipped under the door will quiet him at once. It reassures him that he has not been abandoned for good.

When the veterinarian explains that a house skunk needs not one vaccination but two, one in each hip (the first for canine distemper and the second for feline distemper), and suggests that you might as well get both of them over with today, a bit of bacon will make the perfect award for valor.

When you step back from the kitchen sink without looking and tromp on a black-velvet paw the size of a thimble, it is bacon that will bring the best comfort. Or when you return, breathless, from the All-School Pet Show, flanked by two proud children and clutching a fistful of ribbons and an armful of lunging skunk, it is bacon that will serve as the Triple Champion's real prize.

And when you are about to leave for a country week end, and the suitcases are packed and the children are finally ready and your husband is waiting impatiently in the car and there is no little skunk to be found anywhere, it is the lure of bacon, waved temptingly under each bed in turn, that will coax him out of hiding.

Cheddar cheese is a close second, but bacon is best.

Unfortunately, a diet made up exclusively of scraps and leftovers is not an adequate diet for a skunk, not even when supplemented by all the bugs two very skillful girls can capture in a hot July meadow. It does not provide either the high level of protein that he requires or the exceptionally large quantity of Vitamin A.

So I began by setting out, every night before I went to bed, a nice dish of Purr Pride or Feline Favorite or Kitty's Choice in one of the six delicious, pet-approved flavors, unconditionally guaranteed to provide balanced nutrition for that special cat—and likely to provide a reasonably good basic diet for that special skunk, too, if supplemented with a multi-vitamin-mineral powder. Alice and Anne always added as garnish a few choice morsels from their own plates.

We soon discovered that while pieces of leftover fried shrimp were very acceptable, Kit-Kat's Seafood Supreme was not. The Vita-Rich Veal Banquet was, it seemed, inedible, but the remainder of yesterday's veal and rice casserole was a gourmet skunk's delight.

Yes, we did try dog food but it was just as unsuccessful, and the half-empty cans were so large that they cluttered up the refrigerator. We went back to cat food.

Anne dug out her beloved A. A. Milne books and read to us again the story of Tigger's arrival in the forest and all the troubles poor old Pooh had in finding out just what tiggers like to eat. Certainly our own situation wasn't as grim as that. Our newcomer liked quite a few things—but most of them were sweets or snacks.

Alice pointed out sympathetically that nobody wants to eat only what's good for him and how would we feel if people gave us nothing but liver and spinach. (Myself, I would be delighted, as I love them both, but this eccentricity is not shared by the rest of my family.) The trouble with commercial pet foods, in Alice's opinion, was that they contained too many vitamins to taste good.

Jim remarked that he had always heard that skunks were like raccoons—born rummagers in garbage cans, who would eat anything. If this were indeed true, then our skunk had to be ill.

As for me, I opened yet another brand of cat food and set it down by the back-kitchen radiator.

What we did not realize in those days is that a skunk's appetite is seasonal. If we had started planning his basic diet in the fall rather than in the summer, we would not have had so many problems.

The choosy gourmet of early July becomes an indiscriminate gourmand in late September and a ravenous gorger by mid-November. In December, when he has stuffed himself to bursting as preparation for the long sleep of winter, he becomes finicky again, pokes crossly at his regular food, and is interested mainly in delicacies —and very small nibbles of these.

During the coldest season, when he spends most of his time sleeping, he comes out only briefly to see if there is anything around worth eating. Usually he decides there isn't and grumbles back to bed.

With the first thaw, however, he emerges thin and nervous and heads straight for the table. Now he is ready to eat anything and everything. This gargantuan appetite holds steady (except perhaps for a week or two during the mating season in late February or early March, when other interests predominate) until hot weather; then again it flags. And so the seasonal cycle begins once more.

It is the major cycle of a skunk's life, far more important to him than sex or reproduction. Eating is his main interest, finding food his main occupation (except, of course, for sleeping). We did not know it during those first weeks of summer, but before long our chief difficulty would be not in coaxing our new pet to eat but rather in keeping him from overdoing it. Which is a delicate business with a skunk, since he is apt to feel that if you don't give him that bit of toast he is demanding, you probably don't love him.

A wild skunk's diet is perfectly balanced both as to content and quantity. As he trundles along on his nightly rounds, he finds something tasty on almost every bush and under every stone.

Each season brings its special delicacies. In early summer, during the peak of the insect season, he dines on beetles and bugs of all kinds, sometimes spiced with a few bees, which he can crunch down with casual disregard of the stinger.

Later, when the dry August fields are alive with crickets and grasshoppers, these form the major part of his diet. He likes turtle eggs as well, and an occasional mouse if he can catch one, but bugs and beetles are his mainstay in summer. Salt-crisp and oily, they provide a diet high in protein and rich in vitamins.

As cold weather approaches, the wild skunk adds nuts, leaves, grains, and berries, as well as worms and grubs and sometimes carrion. For a special treat he stands on tiptoe to lick up the moths that are laying eggs on the bark of tree trunks. His portly little figure now becomes positively rotund as he accumulates fat and builds up stamina for the long winter ahead.

At this season, his steadily growing hunger may even drive him to investigate your garbage can or the fringes of the town dump. Since he lacks the raccoon's manual dexterity, he has to pass up any closed container, but whatever lies on the ground is sure to be sampled. Melon rinds, chicken bones, stale bread crusts—all will fit his menu.

Folklore has it that a skunk's autumnal craving for food may even lead him into the barnyard and straight to the poultry house. Accordingly, there are farmers who will shoot a skunk on sight. However, when the U.S. Department of Agriculture examined the stomach contents of some 1,700 skunks, it was found that more than half the material consisted of insects—mainly crickets, grasshoppers, and beetles. The remainder was made up of fruit, grain, and small mammals. There was no evidence of raids on the chicken coop. Perhaps farmers mistakenly blame the skunk for damage actually done by his cousins, the weasel and the mink.

Our skunk did have a passion for chicken, it must be admitted, but he liked it fried. Moreover, I cannot think that any skunk would go to all the trouble of capturing a large, loud, frantic hen unless he were on the brink of starvation, a most unlikely occurrence in view of the available insect population. And even if, through some dire emergency, he were impelled to approach the poultry house, he would be deterred by any properly installed fence.

Instead of reaching for his gun, a farmer should welcome the sight of that small black-and-silver figure ambling out of the shadows. Unlike the raccoon, rabbit, and woodchuck who may also be nearby, this visitor is not thinking of corn or lettuce. His mind is all on the delicious assortment of caterpillars and beetles and grubs he expects to find.

Ernest Thompson Seton once rhapsodized that every

skunk is the guardian angel of a half acre of garden. And so he is—provided that nobody takes after him with a shotgun. Or sets out a trap or a batch of poisoned grain. And also provided that the resident insects haven't been freshly sprayed with DDT or a similar mixture!

All autumn long the happy gorging goes on. When snow comes, the wild skunk is ready. Sleek and round, he curls up in a snug den to sleep away the winter. It is not a true hibernation: occasionally, on a very mild day, he may bestir himself long enough to root for a few worms. But mostly he stays tucked up until the spring thaw rouses all the small sleepers—and the first caterpillars begin to appear.

Apart from man-made hazards, obtaining a well-balanced diet is no problem at all for a wild skunk. Nor does he have a weight problem. If he stuffs himself too much in the fall, he simply sleeps longer in the winter, until all the excess fat has been burned up. There is no danger that he will face the next hot season with bulging sides and rolls of fat around his neck.

Like his brother in the woods, the house skunk has a passionate—you might say a consuming—interest in food. But he does not have to forage all night to complete a single meal. There are no rocky ledges to scramble over on the way to the kitchen. For him, that especially delicious tidbit is more apt to be found on someone's plate than underneath a heavy log. So his actual diet must be curtailed to suit life indoors, although his appetite is still geared to life outdoors.

A fondness for overeating is not his only problem, however. For long periods of time he may become attached to one particular food to the exclusion of all others. (This is a curious aberration in house skunks that can have no counterpart in wild skunks, who have to take what they can get.) He may even turn vicious if given too much raw meat—or so the petshop owner warned us. (It is not always easy to separate fact from fiction when it comes to wild-animal behavior.) Then too, as his appetite changes with the seasons, last month's craving for greens may give way this month to a hunger for starches. Thus his owner is often stranded with an oversupply of whatever food was the-day-before-yesterday's favorite and is at a total loss as to what the current preference might be.

We did not know any of this when we got our own skunk.

As we watched our new baby picking gloomily at his cat food, our main worry was malnutrition, perhaps even starvation. So I began to add bribes—bits of Cheddar, or a sprinkle of buttered toast crumbs. Or a curl of bacon, tucked into the middle like a buried treasure. And the little skunk, after diligent attempts to scrape off the part he didn't like, would give up and eat the whole thing—even with a vitamin-mineral powder on top.

By the end of July, this particular skirmish in the Battle of Human vs. Skunk seemed to have ended in victory for my side.

In later months, however, I became less certain who was the true winner. I found, to be sure, that I could force myself to ignore the most piteous scratching at the kitchen door; I might even open the door and still go about my business, wearing snow boots for protection against ankle nips. And as I mixed his daily meal, I calculated carefully what percentage was nourishment and what percentage reward.

In spite of all this, he grew much too fat—so fat that at times he had to sleep on his back, four paws in the air. It looked very comical but meant that he had become too heavy to sleep comfortably on his stomach.

Whenever this happened, we instituted stern prohibitions against between-meal snacks for him. But unfortunately, as is so often the case, adopting a rule proved easier than observing it. The faintest click of the opening refrigerator door would be enough to rouse him from the soundest sleep in the farthest corner of the house and send him scurrying down the hall to poke a hopefully sniffing nose against the nearest human foot. Only a hardhearted miser could refuse such a pathetic, starving creature.

If no tidbits were forthcoming, he would try scratching. He would hook his claws into a stocking or trouser fabric and then pull: Attention must be paid!

If such desperate efforts were also ignored, a famished skunk's patience could not be expected to last. With his needle-sharp teeth, he would seize a skirt, an apron string, or a pants leg. The sound of ripping cloth would always elicit a response.

But if the response turned out to be merely a furious shout—"Stop that! It is NOT your suppertime!"—he had one last resource, which he now felt fully justified in using: his bite.

Skunks seldom use their teeth in self-defense. (They don't need to, after all.) And they never attack.

They are by nature peace-loving souls, who would always rather back away from trouble than face it (although this is not, perhaps, an accurate statement, since a skunk *faces* danger by turning his back on it). At any rate, a skunk is not apt to slash out with his teeth the way a fox, for instance, might do.

Nevertheless, our skunk did bite us—quite often, in fact. Before he was a year old, he had developed a veritable repertoire of bites, ranging from the tentative nibble which reminded, "Haven't you noticed? I'm here and I'm ravenous!" to the irritable snap which meant, "Go away and let me sleep!" or else, "Why have you kept me waiting so long?"—and finally the real chomp, the genuine bite which expressed fury. This last involved deliberately fastening his teeth and giving a shake, after which he would let go and peer up to see whether he had made himself clear.

It was a limited vocabulary, but an effective one.

So you could not say that skunks are biters in the usual sense—only that they sometimes express themselves with their teeth.

Whenever a skunk feels that he is being unjustly treated—as when someone is slicing ham and not giving him any—he may make his protest felt with a well-placed bite. He has lost patience and that is that.

At which point, however, his human oppressor may also lose patience and decide to shut him up somewhere. But since it is easier to pick up a snapping turtle than an irate baby skunk, the only alternative is to lure him away—with a bit of bacon, perhaps, or a slice of Cheddar.

And so he wins his tidbit at last.

VI

BEING NAGGED BY A HUNGRY SKUNK was no problem during those first weeks. It was the beginning of August, and our new pet had not begun to make friends with us, much less bite us. We hadn't even decided what to name him.

We had, however, reached an agreement with him on a few important house rules—such as where to go to the bathroom.

Skunks have an inborn sense of neatness and order. Their fur is always immaculate; their claws are polished. Their dens are equally neat and clean. A mother will conscientiously seek out a new nest for each litter (with the result that internal parasites are almost never found in the young).

In the woods, skunks go about their rounds as if on schedule, appearing at the same place at almost the same time every night. They seem to have a sort of mental cupboard inventory of just what belongs where and freeze with instant suspicion if they come upon a newly fallen branch, an unfamiliar scatter of leaves, or a rock lying across a formerly clear path. Skunks are firm believers in the old-fashioned housekeeping dictum, "A place for everything and everything in its place."

They are equally precise when it comes to defecation. The usual procedure is to back into a discreet corner, then scratch a sanitary covering of leaves over the spot, and finally scoot along the ground using the grass and moss as toilet paper.

House-training such an animal should be easy, since his own natural inclinations are so closely in accord with human requirements.

"A skunk is a very clean-living animal," our veterinarian informed us.

The pet-shop owner concurred. "Your average skunk," he assured us, "practically house-trains himself."

Which may be true of *his* average skunk.

Certainly the recommended system could not be simpler. In any new environment, a skunk will quickly select a preferred spot—usually a corner—for defecation. Once he has established his preference, you cover the area with newspapers or set up a cat-litter pan there. After he has grown used to this, you have only to transfer the papers or pan to whatever place you yourself have selected and the skunk will follow along.

Unless, of course, his liking for his chosen corner is stronger than for newspapers or cat litter. A good corner, after all, has much to recommend it. It is quiet and private. Also, nothing can creep up on you from behind. A patch of newspapers, on the other hand, or a pan of unnatural-smelling sand, offers neither privacy nor security—especially if it has an alarming habit of suddenly vanishing and then reappearing in a totally new spot.

It is really not so surprising that a baby skunk might regard house-training paraphernalia with suspicion. At least, ours did.

True to expectation, he picked out a favorite corner almost at once. Unfortunately, this was exactly in the angle between two of the most important doors in the back kitchen, the door leading outside and the one leading into the regular kitchen. By day this was the junction of the most heavily trafficked routes in the house, which could prove to be a problem later on if the little skunk gave up his nocturnal schedule. In addition, the area was too small to accommodate his beautiful new turquoise cat pan or even a very big swatch of the *Times* or the *Newtown Bee*. (Since he tended to back himself tight against the wall, the baseboard, as well as the floor, had to be covered.)

Actually, none of the corners in the back kitchen was what might be called an ideal place, from the human point of view, but the corner near the birdseed cupboard (which was now securely wired shut) would be the least inconvenient. All we had to do was to persuade him to transfer from one corner to the other.

By now it was clear that building barricades was not the answer. But a skunk's nose is highly sensitive. Perhaps smell would be a good training aid.

Hoping to attract him to the approved corner, we covered the floor with already used papers. There was no question but that they did smell. However, the lure was ignored.

Then we tried to make the other corner as unattractive

as possible. We sprayed it with "Doggy Do-Not!" and "Off!" and even insect repellent. The back kitchen not only looked like a town dump; it was beginning to smell like one.

Strong odors, however, are no deterrent to a skunk, as we perhaps should have known in advance. Unperturbed, he continued to use his favorite corner between the doors.

Then Jim had a stroke of pure inspiration. He opened both of the doors, back to back, and fixed them in this position by looping Anne's old jump rope around the knobs. And presto!—*the corner was gone.*

This brilliant stratagem worked. When his special nook disappeared, the little skunk had no choice but to retreat to the other corner. Moreover, after a few days he seemed to grow resigned to the new location—which was fortunate because a streak of rainy weather made it imperative to close the outside door again.

When the original corner reappeared, we piled it high with hefty rocks, just in case. They would not stop him from using the area if he were determined to; they would, however, make it inconvenient. But although the rocks were shoved around a bit every night, they did not seem to be needed. The habit that drew him to the new place had finally become established. Eventually, the rocks were discarded.

For a long time afterward, however, whenever he was angry he defiantly returned to his old spot in the long-prohibited corner to leave a token of his displeasure.

Unfortunately, the house-training rules agreed on during that first summer in the country did not hold fast when we returned to the city in the fall.

By then the little skunk fully understood the appropriate use of an array of newspapers on the floor. To say that he understood the system, however, is not to say that he approved of it. He used the correct corner in the country because it was easy. In the city, where we established a new paper-spot in the pantry, it was another matter. He would go there if he happened to be near the pantry to begin with—but if he happened to be snoozing in Alice's bedroom, or nosing among the toys in Anne's closet, or toasting himself by the radiator in Jim's study, the long trek to the pantry was just too much trouble. How much more sensible and convenient to have a special corner in every room of the house! The fact that humans might object seemed quite irrelevant.

Still, he eventually settled down to abiding by the rules most of the time. If he did not, and if he got caught, he would hang his head and dive under the nearest bed—knowing perfectly well that he had broken the rule but obviously feeling that it was a stupid rule.

Frequent puddling became another chronic problem in the city. He was not marking the boundaries of his private territory; he simply urinated whenever and wherever the need arose. This occurred most often in the kitchen, where he became so utterly involved in thoughts of food that he was unconscious of anything else.

We learned to recognize the look. "There he goes again! Grab him!" It was almost always too late.

We might have done better if we could have invented an effective method of punishment, but disciplining a skunk is no easy matter. You must not strike him in anger, for he may never forgive you. Skunks have been known to carry a grudge for life. The most you can do is whack the floor near him with a rolled newspaper, or else—the method

I myself favor—screech at him at the top of your lungs. Skunks cannot abide loud noises and this will at least make him pay attention for a moment.

But even shouting is far from effective. A scolded skunk may droop and look embarrassed. But not very. And not for long. Penitence is not a skunk's style.

It may be that our particular skunk was unusually stubborn or unusually obtuse. I have heard of a lady who paper-trained a pet rabbit and then was given a baby skunk, whereupon the rabbit trained the skunk. What is more, both animals became so conscientious that they hurried to use any stray piece of newspaper that happened to drop to the floor. (This, at least, is the story.)

Perhaps that's what we needed from the very beginning —the help of a nice, conscientious cottontail.

VII

Our summer eased along. There were horseback rides and picnics and the first wild blueberries. Once the Clarks took us sailing on Lake Quassapaug.

The amber pond water, spring fed, slowly warmed from glacial to endurable, so that even I could enjoy the swimming.

The lyrical outburst of spring blossoming that had welcomed us in June subsided with the last of the lilacs, and the field flowers in the girls' bouquets now had comfortable old-fashioned names like heal-all and feverfew, bouncing Bet and yellow loosestrife. And of course, daisy, the day's eye.

It was not all perfection, to be sure. The girls collected sixteen beer cans in a single morning from the roadside near our mailbox (yet cars are so rare along our road that we expect visitors if we hear one coming). And the town fathers voted in favor of a bond issue to finance highway expansion and to set up a commission to study "the means of fostering industrial development" in this blessedly undeveloped valley. But for our own family, the days were idyllic.

Alice was doing research on common New England wild flowers, sometimes with dismaying results: Who would have dreamed that a cheerful flower like blueweed might also be called viper's bugloss? Or that lupines could be poisonous to cattle? But we were proud to learn that our own land sheltered six Endangered Species and that all of them were flourishing.

Anne caught a very thin, small mother leech, who had a cluster of threadlike babies riding on her back as she undulated around a teacupful of water. A gentle poke with a pencil tip would dislodge them, and then they would swim frantically after her until they were all safely attached again. For a while the girls were tempted to keep this odd little family, but they finally decided against it. After all, how would you feed a pet bloodsucker?

One of the high points of the summer was the day we saw a magnificent tiger swallowtail resting on the darkest pine at the far end of the pond, dramatic even at that distance with his boldly shaped wings and blazing color. I thought of Blake, but the girls raced for sketch pad and crayons before there was time to assemble a quotation.

Another unforgettable moment came when I got up one night and paused at the window to admire the wash of moonlight across the back yard. Suddenly, out of the shadows, moving pale and silent like the ghost of some long-extinct wild pig, there came trotting a huge opossum.

He was a giant, long-legged and bony, and he crossed purposefully over to the house to check the garbage can and the back doorstep. I had always imagined a possum as a sort of sloth, clambering heavily along a branch—dim-witted, nearsighted, and festooned with babies. But there was nothing slow or pathetic about this efficient night raider. Before I could move to waken the children, he was gone.

We discovered a pair of hawks nesting in the old butternut tree. And a raccoon began to fish our pond: every morning we found a fresh set of starprints in the mud.

One day Alice looked out her window and discovered, strung across a lilac that brushed her sill, the perfect, crystal-fretted web of one of the orb-weaving spiders. In the center sat the weaver herself, handsomely marked in black and yellow and fully as large as a lima bean. She was also a cripple—one of her front legs was gone.

The girls looked her up and found that she was an Argiope. It rhymes with Calliope, so they looked *her* up too, hoping that she would also be a weaver, one of those three Fates of Greek mythology who spin the web of human existence—but instead she turned out to be the muse of eloquence and epic poetry.

The Argiope spider, the girls learned, would stay on her web all summer, then in September would lay her eggs in a neat pear-shaped cocoon, rather like a tiny brown paper bag. In October she would disappear, probably dying in one of the early frosts.

"Poor thing!" said Anne. "Such a short life! And crippled, too."

"Let's name her!" Alice suggested. "And feed her some mosquitoes."

We still had not been able to find the right name for our poor little skunk, but the girls had no trouble at all in naming their spider. They called her Argiope Jane and raced down to the pond to catch her some breakfast.

Then there was the evening when Jim was driving up from New York and saw twin fawns standing right at the edge of the parkway, in the middle of suburban Westchester.

There was plenty of wildlife to be observed that summer outside our house. Inside it, however, our resident specimen remained all but invisible.

He was now eating his proper supper, vitamin-mineral powder and all, and he had consented to use the papers in the correct corner most of the time. Yet after weeks of living in our home, this little, nameless newcomer was still as much of an outsider as ever: a mere shadow under the radiator by day and an unseen poltergeist in the back kitchen by night.

Something had to be done. I thought back to Alice's remark that a pet should be rewarding.

Remembering our first success, when the remnants of Anne's sandwich had lured the baby skunk from his lair under the washing machine, we decided to try a similar approach this time. We would bribe him with his favorite tidbits: scraps of bacon and pieces of Cheddar cheese. But now our aim would be to win his trust—even, perhaps, his friendship.

And so the nightly vigils began.

Alice and Anne drew lots for the first night and took turns thereafter. Each night, one of them would sit patiently on the floor near the radiator, holding a tempting bait on her lap. When at length she was overcome by prickling legs and numbness in the toes, plus an unquenchable desire to sneeze, I would take her place. My own endurance was limited: I seldom lasted more than fifteen minutes.

Meanwhile, there would be the sound of much sniffing under the radiator and occasionally a glimpse of that blackberry nose, twitching excitedly. But the little skunk's sense of caution seemed to outweigh his appetite. Emerging from his den to whisk up scraps from the kitchen floor was one thing; venturing onto someone's lap was quite another.

"Give him time," my mother wrote from Cape Cod. "Remember, he's only a baby."

We realized this, but even so, the whole business was becoming thoroughly discouraging.

"Why don't you try cutting down on his regular meals?" Jim suggested one evening as he hoisted me up from the kitchen floor.

"I don't know. That would be awfully hard on him."

"But isn't all this rather hard on you?"

True. So the following night I set out only half the usual portion of Kitty's Choice.

When Anne settled on the floor for the next "watch hour" (it happened to be her turn that evening) and the delicious smell of Cheddar cheese and bacon wafted under the radiator, the nose appeared instantly. After only a moment's hesitation, it was followed by a small, silver-streaked head and then by our pet himself, a mere wisp of body and a magnificent plume of tail. A single flash, and both skunk and snack were gone.

The rest was easy. Not that our progress could be called *rapid*, you understand, but at least it was steady.

The next evening, he came out more confidently. Before long, he was accepting his tidbits directly from the hand. One evening he paused as he was scrabbling over Alice's knee, lifted his head, and gazed earnestly up into her face. It was his first sign of recognition that he was dealing with another living creature, not merely a food-bearing hill of some sort.

At last the time came when he would eat his snack right on the donor's lap instead of snatching it back to his den. He was always poised for flight, however. The slightest movement, the least inadvertent twitch, and he would vanish again.

Through it all, Alice and Anne were miracles of patience. They learned to curb their flyaway movements and quiet their bubbling giggles. They sat on the kitchen floor like statues during the nightly taming session.

It was very unfair that the ultimate moment of success, when it finally came, was mine.

The girls had gone to bed early that night—or rather, not exactly to bed but to camp out with their sleeping bags in the back yard. They were snugged down under the big Norway spruce, arguing good-naturedly over the names of the stars shining through the branches, and checking and rechecking their supplies:

> Flashlights
> Tissues
> Insect repellent
> Water
> Cookies
> Apples
> Books

They had enough to last a week, but actually neither

camper made it through the night: Alice came in at midnight because the fireflies were too bright; Anne appeared at five because she was sure she heard wolves.

Jim was staying over in New York because it made more sense: he had a 9:00 A.M. meeting the next day.

As a result, I was left with the sole responsibility for that night's skunk-taming session. I took along a few supplies of my own: the inevitable Cheddar and bacon bits, of course, and also two cushions, a paperback novel which could be managed inconspicuously in one hand, and a small glass for occasional sipping when the skunk wasn't looking. Thus equipped, I felt ready to face the tedious job ahead.

I had barely established myself on the floor when the sable face with its single snowy mark came poking out from under the radiator. His whiskers were feathery with dust.

He seemed surprised at not finding one of the girls, since they were usually on duty during the first part of the evening. But he started toward me, picking his way over the slippery floor, nose down, tail drooping in a relaxed curve. Eagerly he sniffed his way over my ankle and up into my lap, where the expected reward was waiting. Ravenously he gobbled it down and then hunted around for more. I was sorry I hadn't brought something extra, the poor little fellow seemed so famished.

But then, suddenly, he stopped his sniffing, laid one tiny paw on my hand, and looked up, up into my face. For a long moment, we regarded each other. Then, with a small, satisfied sigh, the baby skunk circled twice in my lap, settled himself in the coziest spot, and fell instantly asleep.

The next night I was able to lay my hand gently on his

back, and the night after that I picked him up. By the end of the week, he had extended his trust to Alice and Anne as well, and was whisking about the back kitchen at their heels. It took longer for him to accept Jim, who had not been such a steady part of the daily (or nightly) routine, but with time—and numerous scraps of steak and chicken—a kind of wary understanding was achieved between them.

"I think he's really beginning to like us," I reported proudly to my mother during my weekly phone call to the Cape.

"However can you tell," she asked, "with an animal that doesn't purr or wag his tail?"

"Well, you see, if he likes you, he falls asleep in your lap."

Not the most rewarding response, perhaps, but to us it seemed marvelous. Just to hold that trusting little bundle while it slept was a great achievement. He was so light and so still that only a circle of warmth marked his presence.

VIII

By MID-AUGUST, the old house in Connecticut contained two worlds, coexisting on different levels. On one level it was still our familiar summer home, which belonged to us as it had belonged to our parents and grandparents. But on another level it had become a labyrinth of secret trails and private dens and hidden nooks. On this level, it belonged to the little skunk.

The dual existence became obvious on the very first evening we opened the back-kitchen door and allowed him into the main house to explore. We all had misgivings. He was, after all, very small for such a big new world. But he was quite tame now, and we thought he deserved an occasional adventure.

At first the open door startled him. He paused on the threshold and flared his tail, ready to thump a warning if necessary. Everything was quiet. He sniffed and caught the reassuringly familiar smell of humans and of food.

Food! He dropped his nose to the floor and scurried straight as a homing pigeon across to the kitchen garbage pail.

"Watch it!" shouted Anne, bounding after him.

Too late. There was a crash as the container tipped over, spilling its contents helter-skelter onto the freshly mopped floor. A moment later a blissful baby skunk was deep in macaroni.

Nobody could have asked for a more dramatic beginning.

When he was finally extracted from his unscheduled feast, our small explorer turned his attention to the rest of the house. Nose down, he bustled along the walls from room to room. Intent, totally absorbed, he seldom paused and never turned back. Later we came to realize that during this single tour he had established for himself a mental map, probably based on smell since his eyesight was poor: a sort of olfactory atlas which from then on never failed him. Even if someone carried him, let us say, from a trip in the car to the relatively unfamiliar downstairs bedroom and set him in the farthest corner, he was never lost or confused. No matter which room he might be in, he always knew the nearest exit and the shortest way back to the kitchen.

Having mapped his new world, he then went about the business of settling it. In the weeks that followed, the house was quite transformed.

It was not just that heaps of rocks sprouted in prohibited corners. Soon there were little skunk nests everywhere: under Anne's bed, behind Alice's door, in my closet, and of course under the back-kitchen radiator. Each had its cozy pile of shredded paper (filched from wastebaskets), plus odds and ends of treasures that he liked to take to bed with him: old bones, a rubber ball, a stuffed dog, a well-chewed glove (which was not so much chewed, puppy-fashion, as *bitten*, with precise rows of needlelike punctures).

Moreover, an invisible network of trails crisscrossed the house, complete with detours and short cuts. Landmarks were selected, and woe to any chair that was pushed to an unfamiliar spot. It would be thumped at and challenged until the change was corrected. Wastebaskets were bowled over so that they could be used as burrows, and if some unthinking human set one upright again, the little skunk hurried to knock it down once more.

Doors were classified according to what Alice called their openability. There were some which could be opened by a firmly pushing nose; others required clawing at the bottom crack. He always used the correct method for each door. A few (very few in an old house) were completely resistant. With these he undertook a long-term excavation project, digging away persistently at the base as if hoping that eventually he could tunnel right through. In spite of his long claws, he never marred the wood; he merely scratched the paint a little. Of course all this effort often brought the desired result, since the nearest human, driven to distraction by the steady scrape-scrape-scrape, would open the door and let him in.

In every room he selected an emergency hideaway, a dark corner that offered safety if too much was going on in the human world. Many times a guest was startled by a flash of black and white between his feet as the little skunk dived for a favorite retreat underneath the guest's chair. Sometimes the guest had not realized until that moment that we even had a house pet.

By this time our skunk had clearly established himself as a member of the family, but he was still without a name. The girls tended to call him "honey," while I was apt to find myself saying, "Come here now, that's a good little skunklet." Jim usually addressed him as "You, there!" (As in, "You, there! Stay away from that waste-basket!")

One thing we all agreed on: we did not want to give him a name that suggested *smell*. No skunk of ours was going to have an insulting name like Petunia or Sweet Pea.

Jim suggested Mephistopheles, Prince of Darkness. But the girls vetoed this on the grounds that they couldn't pronounce it, much less spell it. They were also against such facetious proposals as Napoleon, Augustus, Mercutio, or, simply, Himself. Their father explained that he hadn't intended these as serious suggestions, although he rather liked them, all the same.

I myself favored naming our skunk Shadow, because he was small and dark and always at somebody's heels. But again the girls objected. "Too spooky," said Anne, and her sister agreed. Perhaps shadows still held for them some memory of terror lingering from the bad dreams of early childhood.

My mother came down from Cape Cod for a brief visit, and it was her opinion that we should call him Earnest, "because that's what he is— just look at that little face!" But this name somehow reminded us of a farm dog.

The children drew up lists—Slipper, Scamper, Moon-light, Firefly, Sniffy, Trinket, Silvertip, even the mundane

Blackie—but none of the possibilities seemed quite right.

The scientific designation turned out to be *Mephitis mephitis* (*mephitis* meaning "noxious vapor"—doubled!) and the Algonquian Indian name, from which the word "skunk" is derived, was *seganku* (we've no idea what that one means). We didn't feel that we could cope with either of these.

In the end, the little skunk's own nature and habits suggested the right name for him. And when we tried it out, he recognized it at once.

It all happened because a thirteen-year-old neighbor came over one day to take some animal pictures. Davy was an excellent photographer, who had just completed a thoroughly professional "photo feature" on rural fairs for the *Lakeville Journal*. We were suitably honored to have him offer his services to us.

He arrived draped with equipment and immediately began surveying the house for all the best picture locations. He tilted lamps and rearranged furniture and pinned up a sheet to serve as a backdrop for close-ups. When everything was ready, he turned to me and said, "All right. Where is he?"

Where indeed? Ordinarily at that hour a sensible house skunk would still be sleeping. But we had made a point of waking ours in midafternoon to be sure that he would be ready to have his picture taken. Alice had given him several nice pieces of bacon and then Anne had raced him around the house to put him in a playful mood. However, in the excitement of Davy's arrival, we had forgotten him just long enough.

We searched, as the saying goes, high and low—mainly low. We crawled around peering under every bed and chair and chest. The skunk had simply vanished. ("Why don't you name him Houdini?" Davy said.)

We tried calling, too—"Here, little skunk! Here, skunk!" —but without results. The photographer checked his watch; there was another assignment waiting.

"It's not that he's unfriendly," Anne explained to Davy. "He's not hiding because he doesn't want to meet you. It's just that he likes to be *secret*."

"Then what's he doing chewing up my Nikon strap?" Davy asked. Sure enough, there he was, cautiously sampling the leather strap which was dangling over the edge of the armchair.

We never found the secret hiding place he used that day. But we had found a name for him.

Ruler of secret trails and hidden nests; inventor of private games which kept him racketing around half the night; planner of surreptitious assaults on garbage pail and refrigerator—this small animal cherished secrecy above all else. And when, for the first time, we called, "Here, Secret!" he came at once.

Months later a visitor congratulated us on choosing such an appropriate name for a skunk. "Just like the new deodorant, how clever!" We had never heard of the product, but we soon discovered that lots of people had. By then, however, it was too late to change. So Secret he remained, or sometimes Seekie, which wasn't too bad either, since seeking (mostly for food) was one of his favorite pastimes.

IX

THE GOLDENROD BEGAN TO DARKEN into bronze and overnight a single scarlet branch blazed out in the marsh. Argiope Jane disappeared, her bed destroyed by a heavy thunderstorm: she never had a chance to make the egg cocoon we were hoping to see. The first of our neighbor's sweet corn arrived and so did the first school announcements—class assignments and health forms and the calendar for the upcoming year. New York obligations, which had seemed so remote, began to reassert their city urgency. Before long, our country summer would be over.

It was time to begin preparing ourselves for the move back to New York. But this year, city life would be far different for us because our skunk would be part of it. What is more, Secret was now four months old. In another two months he would be fully grown—and the older he grew, the more self-assertive he became.

He had long since outgrown his baby bed under the

radiator and had appropriated the broom closet instead, evicting the vacuum cleaner, two brooms, and assorted mops as well as the ironing board. He was, in fact, the perfect size for his splendid cage, but keeping him in captivity was of course unthinkable. I did put his dishes in the cage, since this made for easier cleaning when he dumped out something he didn't like.

Alice made a chart for the bulletin board to help us keep track of all the new skunk-related chores that had been added to our housekeeping.

At least we no longer needed to step around any barricades. The rocks and books were gone: he was much too fat to slither under the bookcase or squeeze through the crack in the closet door. Besides, he had lost interest in exploring forbidden areas. His routes had been established and he seldom deviated from them.

The inevitable September move to New York would be hard on Secret, we knew. For that matter, it would be hard on us too! But when the time came, the trip itself was easy: we left the country in the middle of the day and he slept through most of it.

He roused himself as we carried him up in the elevator, however, and began to struggle wildly to escape. We got our door unlocked just as seven pounds of furious skunk tore himself loose.

He whizzed down the entry hall, swerved sharply into the nearest bedroom, and plunged to safety under the bed. Here he stayed for the rest of the day, refusing to be coaxed out. It was not until suppertime that the combination of hunger and curiosity finally induced him to find his way to the kitchen; once there, he glowered at

LIST OF CLEANING UP SKUNK

	MON.	TUES.	WED.	THURS.	FRI.	SAT.	SUN.
ALICE	SWEEP-ING	WASHING OUT HIS DISHES	CLEAN-ING HIS CAGE	SWEEP-ING	WASHING OUT HIS DISHES	CLEAN-ING HIS CAGE	SWEEP-ING
ANNE	WASHING OUT HIS DISHES	CLEAN-ING HIS CAGE	SWEEP-ING	WASHING OUT HIS DISHES	CLEAN-ING HIS CAGE	SWEEP-ING	WASHING OUT HIS DISHES
MOM	BATH-ROOM WORK	BATH-ROOM WORK	BATH-ROOM WORK	BATH-ROOM WORK	BATH-ROOM WORK	BATH-ROOM WORK	BATH-ROOM WORK

the strange garbage container, and whirled and thumped when I dropped a fork.

It took him several days to settle down. He distrusted this new place with its unaccustomed noises and unfamiliar smells. And he disliked the new routines which city living imposed on us all: meals came at unexpected hours and people never seemed to be where they should be.

A puppy would have found it easier to make the change. Any place is home to a dog if his beloved humans are there. Even a kitten—devoted though cats are to an orderly routine—would have managed to adjust fairly soon. The cat may walk by himself, but as a rule he is amenable to walking in the same general direction as the humans he lives with.

But here again, as in so many other ways, a skunk is not like a domestic pet. He insists on choosing his own trail and will not deviate from it even slightly to accommodate somebody else. What is more, anyone wishing to do business with him had better fall in line.

So when Secret set himself to the task of turning this new environment into the proper sort of habitat for a skunk, we found ourselves forced to go along. In a word, we adjusted.

After a few weeks he had explored all the alien territory, finding new trails and establishing new hiding places. He had classified all the doors, become reconciled to a new den in the pantry, and discovered a splendid place for napping beside the radiator in Jim's study. (Originally intended as a maid's room, I suppose—for a midget-sized maid—this so-called study barely accommodates Jim's typewriter table, a bookcase, and a very narrow desk. It challenged all Secret's skill at stuffing himself into small spaces for him to work out a satisfactory resting place, halfway under the desk and right next to the hottest radiator in the house.)

When he was done, the city apartment was as much like the country house as he could make it. And the latter, of course, had long since been transformed to suit his own tastes and requirements.

Inevitably, many of these rearrangements were rather inconvenient for us, but we were learning what it takes to live successfully with a house skunk: compromise. As time went on, Secret was growing more set in his ways; we, however, were growing more flexible in ours. We were, in fact—both skunk and family—approaching a state of household harmony.

As I look back on all the adjustments we went through during Secret's first summer with us in Connecticut and that first autumn and winter in New York, as he was growing from featherlight infancy to a full twelve pounds of maturity, I can see that a basic pattern of life was slowly taking shape: habits and attitudes were crystallizing into that clear predictability which a skunk cherishes so highly.

As a fully adult skunk, Secret continued to resent change as stubbornly as he had when he was a baby. He snapped at anyone who awakened him at an unaccustomed hour and threatened any carton or suitcase unexpectedly encountered while making his rounds. The broom became his sworn enemy because it was forever thrusting itself under beds and sweeping out his beloved nests. He found no consolation in the fact that a new nest could be made in a matter of minutes, and I don't entirely blame him. After all, when you get a place fixed up just the way you like it, you naturally object to having it disrupted.

His daily schedule was equally fixed. Like a fussy old man, he found security in the undeviating observance of domestic ritual. He roused himself every morning just as the breakfast bacon began to sizzle, and he scratched steadily at the kitchen door until he was admitted for a snack.

Whenever we were trying to put him on a crash diet, we had to forego having bacon ourselves, since the sound and smell of frying would awaken him instantly. He could sleep through eggs and cereal, provided that we walked on tiptoe and spoke only in whispers. The idea of four people sneaking around like burglars in their own kitchen so as not to arouse one skunk may seem downright absurd, I can only say that the idea of the same four people happily munching their breakfast while a poor little animal is clearly dying of starvation just outside their door is downright cruel.

After his morning snack, he usually trundled back to bed and would not be seen again until late afternoon.

Secret's nocturnal schedule proved to have certain advantages as far as we were concerned. We could go about our own affairs all day without feeling guilty that we were neglecting a bored, lonely house pet. On the other hand, it did mean that during the dinner hour and all through the evening, we could count on plenty of company. And this was precisely the time when we liked to relax, unwind, and not have to play tag with a skunk.

My only consolation was to reflect that one can't have everything and that probably a nocturnal pet was best suited to our busy lives.

Our evenings became undeniably skunk-centered.

I solved the dinnertime hassle by feeding Secret just as we sat down to our own meal. By the time he had polished his dish, cleaned his nose and paws, and taken his postprandial nap, we ourselves had finished in peace.

But then he woke up, full of energy and ready to make a night of it. If we were in the country, someone took him for an outing in the yard. If we were in the city, someone had to chase him around the apartment for at least an hour of hard play. Usually that pleasure fell to me.

Among the many after-dinner games he invented that first winter was to hide around a corner or under a bed and pounce out at passing feet, or to chase and be chased up and down the long hallway. Attacking a string was another favorite game, and so was wrestling with a stuffed animal or with someone's stoutly gloved hand. This last game can be hazardous, since your fellow player may roll over on his back when you least expect it, holding the glove in his teeth and grasping your hand with surprisingly strong paws so that you cannot pull free, and then suddenly abandon the glove and lunge for your wrist. No hostility is involved—baby skunks play this way with one another—but even the friendliest bite can be formidable if you don't have a protective thickness of fur.

A vigorous romp, whether indoors or out, always left Secret puffing for breath, and he was happy to be lifted onto someone's lap for a snooze.

It is curiously relaxing to read or watch television with a lapful of sleeping skunk. He is warm as a muff (though perhaps this is not the happiest simile for a refugee from a fur farm) and cozy as a pillow. His coat is very soft, the undercoat fine and pure as eiderdown, the long outer guard hairs shining like black satin. The broad white stripe glistens.

He seldom stirs in his sleep. With a wild animal's selective hearing, he ignores telephone bells and fire sirens and dropped roller skates. Yet he wakes instantly if something snaps like a breaking twig or creaks softly like branches in the wind, and he often reacts to sounds that are inaudible to human ears. This aural acuteness is surprising, since a skunk's ears are so small—mere petals folded inconspicuously against his head.

But in the evening, such naps are short. Secret would seldom sleep for more than half an hour; then he would rear up, ready to go again. Sliding to the floor, he would scamper to the center of the room, wheel about, and drum out his challenge: "Catch me if you can! I dare you to try!" With each beat, he made a small backward hop. The correct response was to stand up, give a couple of answering hops, and then stamp out a triple beat of your own. "Ready or not—here I come!"

After this second round of fun and games, Secret would be ready for a second nap. We learned that this was the time to lure him to his bed. We gave him a slice of cheese or scrap of bacon by way of consolation, set out his toys, and firmly latched the door. For the rest of the night, he would have to manage by himself as best he could.

His main problem of adjustment arose if we were busy in the evening. Perhaps the girls had homework to do or a very exciting chapter to finish reading, and Jim and I had theater tickets or a dinner invitation. In such cases, poor Secret found that he had to shift for himself. He would gloom about the house, scratching at doors and trying to entice someone into a game. As a rule, he tipped over his water dish and dumped the sofa cushions on the floor. He left large puddles in the entry hall. If a neighbor were "sitting" for us, he crouched around a corner and glared at her. Eventually, since skunks are innately sensible souls, he would hide somewhere and go to sleep. At the first familiar footfall, however, he would come boiling out, and it always required a lot of petting and several particularly delicious snacks to make peace.

X

Secret developed what we expect is a typical skunk's view of family holidays. Valentine's Day and the Fourth of July didn't interest him particularly—but Thanksgiving! Not only was there so much going on in the kitchen, but best of all, there were so many unusual treats. "Don't put too much onion in the stuffing," Anne always warned, "or Seekie won't like it."

Birthday parties provided ice-cream dishes to lick and a wonderful sprinkling of cake crumbs all over the floor. Christmas meant an added stocking by the fire, filled with a variety of things that would be fun to sniff: a large pine cone, some sea shells, a handful of dried heather, an old moss-covered root.

But it was Halloween that seemed to be a skunk's idea of the perfect holiday, at least as celebrated at our house. On Halloween even the humans like to have things dark. Also, a lot is happening on the floor where a skunk can join in.

We always spend the holiday in New York, and it is traditional with us for each girl to invite one friend for a Halloween sleep-over. After making the neighborhood rounds and gobbling a hasty supper by candlelight, the four girls turn out all the lamps in the living room and settle down on the floor for magic tricks, ghost stories (provided by Jim), and fortunetelling of every conceivable type: crystal ball, Ouija board, gypsy cards, tea leaves, even Chinese cookies. Both girls are dedicated fortunetellers.

On Secret's first Halloween, our witch, gypsy, Spanish dancer, and lady hobo had scarcely arranged themselves cross-legged in the mystic circle when they heard an odd noise which seemed to be coming closer. "Mom!" the witch called. "What's that noise?" I hurried from the kitchen to investigate.

In the glow of the jack-o'-lantern we saw a fat little skunk come bucketing down the darkened hall. In his mouth he carried the drawstring of a large orange trick-or-treat bag which ballooned above him.

By the living-room door, he caught a familiar scent, dropped his bag, and a moment later plumped down amid the fortunetelling cards.

"Oh, Seekie!" said the gypsy affectionately. "You wanted to come to the party too! Like to have some of these potato chips?"

No need to ask.

Traveling by car is another family activity which a skunk can enjoy, although there was a time when we would never have believed it.

Our first automobile trips with Secret were unbearable,

for him as well as for us. Since we did not have a special carrying case, we transported him in an old guinea-pig cage, made comfortable with newspapers, a few toys and a cracker or two. Within ten minutes after we had started, however, he would become so upset that he lost muscular control—both fore and aft, so to speak. The results are better left undescribed. All I can say is that traveling with a skunk was an ordeal for everyone concerned.

It was Jim who finally solved the problem and in a very simple manner. He threw away the cage and gave Secret the freedom of the car. At once, Secret settled down very happily. Apparently it was the confinement that had been so disturbing. From then on, car trips were always easy.

But that first experiment of Jim's did have one harrowing moment. The girls and I had gone to Cape Cod several days before, leaving to Jim the dubious pleasure of driving up from New York with Secret. In view of the fact that our earlier traveling arrangements had been so unsatisfactory, he decided to try a new approach. After covering the back floor of the car with a thick carpet of newspapers, he cautiously put Secret down to explore. Efficiently the little skunk began sniffing out the possibilities of this strange new area. Not much room back there but a good deal more than in a cage. He seized a corner of the newspaper in his mouth and deftly tore off a long strip. The place might be improved if it had a good nest. Seeing that his small passenger was settling down so well, Jim went back up to the apartment for the rest of the luggage (those few necessities which the girls and I had not taken along: three suitcases, a large bag of groceries, a box of skunk supplies, two music stands, a typewriter, the electric toaster, my favorite coffeepot, Jim's own skin-diving gear, and a carton of records and books). When he returned, Secret was nowhere to be seen.

Jim searched for half an hour before he telephoned the Cape.

"No, I haven't left yet. Yes, I'm still in New York. Look, I don't know how you are going to break this to the girls, but, well—I've lost their skunk. I left him in the car but he must have gotten out somehow. Maybe somebody opened the door."

Lost? In New York City? Amid all those yelling truck-drivers and screeching taxi brakes and shouting pedestrians? It was too awful to imagine.

Besides, how would you go about looking for a lost skunk in a big city? I could imagine the phone call to the local police precinct. "Is this the Missing Persons Bureau? Well, you see, I want to report a lost skunk. That's what I said: *skunk*. S as in secret, k as in king, u as. . . . No, officer, this is NOT my idea of a joke."

"Don't give up yet!" I begged Jim. "Have you gone as far as Riverside Drive? He might have headed toward the park."

"I've done that," Jim said, "but I'll try again. I'll call you back."

When the telephone rang again, a feeling of relief flooded over me even before I lifted up the receiver.

"It's all right," my husband said. "I made one last search of the car and I happened to stick my hand under the back seat. Something licked my fingers."

We had not known (I daresay few people do) that underneath the springs of the back seat there is just enough space for a very determined skunk to squeeze into.

Secret had moved in at once. What is more, he stayed in this improvised skunk den, sleeping contentedly, throughout the entire six-hour drive to Cape Cod.

He eventually outgrew the crevice under the back seat, but he then learned to wedge himself under the front seat, where there was more space, and there he dozed away innumerable trips without a single mishap. He liked the spot so well, in fact, that only a very big snack would entice him out. He also liked to spend part of every trip sprawled across the girls' laps. It was the one time when he could be sure that they wouldn't keep hopping up every few minutes.

From our point of view, he became a perfect traveler: never carsick and never in need of a "rest stop." From his own point of view, there was only one objection to taking a car trip: it always began at such an ungodly hour. (Such as shortly after breakfast.) A skunk would much prefer starting out at midnight.

It was a good thing that Secret was so amenable to car traveling, because we had to do a lot of it after he came to live with us. In addition to our regular week-end and vacation trips to Connecticut and the annual trek to Cape Cod, we found ourselves obliged to make all sorts of extra trips just on Secret's account. The problem was that his doctor happened to be in Connecticut (city veterinarians having proved to be less knowledgeable about skunks), and Secret had to see a good deal of his doctor.

Most pet skunks require little medical attention. They must have a rabies shot, of course, and double distemper inoculations (both feline and canine), as well as an occasional fecal examination to check for internal parasites. But they are noted for their good health.

Poor Secret was the exception. He arrived with a severe case of roundworms. When these were cleared up, we discovered that he had a tapeworm. This was followed by coccidia, a very persistent type of internal parasite. Still other problems developed later.

Each new ailment required another trip to the animal hospital in Connecticut. We became familiar figures in the waiting room, among all the Great Danes lurching at their chains and Siamese cats yowling in their silk-lined cases, as we sat quietly (and, I must confess, a trifle smugly, since *our* patient always behaved beautifully) with a bundle of skunk tucked under our jacket. I say "our jacket" because we took turns holding him: whoever was free could roam around the waiting room getting acquainted with other animals and their owners. The doctor would laugh sympathetically when he saw us. "So here you are again! Well, what seems to be the matter this time?"

Each new ailment also involved a new kind of medication, of course. For weeks on end Secret had to be dosed with pink tablets or yellow tablets or gray tablets, each neatly disguised in a pellet of hamburger. One variety had to be taken four times a day, which meant waking him up at annoying intervals. He moped a good deal, and although he continued to gobble down his food, he sometimes threw it up again almost immediately. It was a long wait until the miracle drugs performed their promised miracles, but at last he seemed to be cured of everything.

Then he developed a mysterious scab on his shoulder, which was unlike any skin disease our veterinarian had ever seen before. A circle of fur was shaved off around the infected spot (the surrounding skin was pink and soft as a baby's) and an evil-smelling ointment applied twice daily. It did not bother Secret as much as it did me.

Fortunately the infection, whatever it was, did not spread and the scab soon healed. But now a new trouble developed. His entire skin started to flake off in unsightly, dandrufflike scales. I inadvertently found a cure for this myself when I decided to add a teaspoon of vinegar and oil salad dressing to his nightly menu. Within a week the dryness had completely disappeared and his fur shone.

The last problem was the worst. It sometimes happens that a skunk's anal muscles are damaged during the descenting operation. If this occurs, the rectum may later slip and protrude from the anus, and the skunk himself is apparently unable to retract it. Theoretically the condition can be corrected within a few days by massage, but Secret's case was complicated by a considerable amount of swelling. We applied an antibiotic salve for several weeks without noticeable effect. In time, however, the condition began to improve. I rather suspect that as he grew older and his muscles became stronger, the problem simply corrected itself.

Throughout these periods of affliction, Secret maintained an air of exemplary stoicism. Even on the doctor's examining table he never struggled or tried to bite; he merely buried his head in the crook of my arm and endured. Fortunately, the rectal trouble was his last. He caught an occasional cold (probably from poking about

Anne.

No interruptions allowed.

Playing footsy.

Whatever it is—it isn't food!

A resourceful skunk makes his burrows where he can.

Summer afternoon beside the pond with Anne and Alice.

among discarded tissues in the wastebasket when some human had a cold) and this caused comical little sneezing fits which appeared to mystify him very much, but otherwise he was ruggedly healthy. The time came when I felt that I could throw away all the leftover pills and tablets and the last of the ointment.

Wild skunks—which have a life expectancy of eight to ten years—do very nicely without miracle medicines. In fact, in areas that have not been invaded by civilization, skunks would multiply like lemmings if it were not for a curious process of natural species control which operates during the mating season.

It sometimes happens that if a male approaches a pregnant female, she will turn on him and bite him. The bite apparently transmits some sort of organism that is toxic to skunks, for no matter where the bite occurs, the victim is likely to develop a severe infection of the lower jaw, which usually proves fatal. Many experts believe that this jaw infection is an important control factor in skunks and accounts for a large percentage of mortality among males.

The wild skunk population is also reduced by an occasional outbreak of rabies. A skunk's lack of fear makes him an easy prey for the bite of a rabid animal. And although the disease does not usually cause in skunks the violent reaction that it may provoke in other animals, it is just as surely fatal.

An even more important cause of death, of course, is the automobile. When a car comes bearing down on him, the skunk's tendency is to face the monster and give it fair warning. But otherwise, he has few enemies. I have heard that the great horned owl will sometimes attack a skunk (in fact, I have read somewhere that an owl once struck a collie which had a white V-shaped marking on its back). Certainly, Secret would grow very uneasy on windy nights, as if sensing that the commotion might mask the sound of wings rushing toward him. Not that he had ever faced an owl, or any other danger, for that matter. But instinct has its own memories.

XI

As OWNERS OF A PET SKUNK, we automatically became experts on all skunks, household and otherwise—or so everyone seemed to consider us. At parties, conferences, and in the elevator, people bore down on us, eager to discuss skunks.

Before long, we had also collected a number of impossible comments, which we learned to endure but not evade, and for which we enjoyed devising impossible replies.

"Good God! A skunk! Has he been deskunked?"

We haven't found out yet.

"Hey! What do you know! That's a skunk you've got there!"

Nope. Porcupine.

"Do I see what I THINK I see?"

That all depends.

In real life, of course, our invariable response to all of these remarks was a weak smile and a polite "Yes."

The one serious question asked most often was, "Are skunks intelligent?" It is a question we ourselves often discussed. On some days Secret's intelligence seemed to be about equal to that of a very bright snail. On other days he outwitted us as expertly as, perhaps, a leopard.

Most of the time, he showed a certain peasant shrewdness which enabled him to function well within a limited scope. In particular, he was extremely competent at finding food, making himself comfortable, and avoiding trouble.

Very playful when in the right mood, he introduced us to skunk versions of hide-and-seek, wrestling, and tag, as well as to such special games as catch-the-snake and bluff-the-enemy (this last a thumping, tail-fanning game which humans are not able to play very well). When he was a baby, he loved to plant his front paws on a slice of toast or a piece of melon rind and go sliding across the kitchen floor. He was also fond of chasing a bottle cap as if it were a bug or, better yet, chasing Anne's bare heels as she went tipping in front of him squeaking "Ticky-ticky-ticky." ("Why in the world do you go 'ticky' at him?" Alice inquired. "Because he likes ·it," Anne said.) Even when he was fully grown, he still insisted on his nightly romp. I am not sure to what extent playfulness is·an indication of animal intelligence, but it is hard to imagine playing games with a guinea pig.

Curiosity skunks have in abundance, but it is always tempered with caution. Whenever Secret would creep up to investigate anything new or strange, he would always pause first to confirm his escape route.

He also displayed a kind of intelligence in his relationship with his human family, recognizing differences among us and adjusting his behavior accordingly.

To be sure, his conception of family roles was distinctly Mid-Victorian.

He treated my husband with the respect due the head of the household. He peered around the door of Jim's study to make certain that it was all right to enter and stayed a safe distance until called. His attitude was distinctly wary and always polite. Yet whenever Jim sat down in the living room to read the evening paper, Secret came clambering up the ramp of outstretched legs to settle proudly on the high chief's lap. And no matter what the situation, he never bit Jim.

He considered Alice rather like a sibling of about his own age. She was the one who could most easily be coaxed into games or persuaded to grant one last tidbit. He loved to be heaved up onto her bed when she was curled among the pillows doing her homework. It was the aim of his life to be able to sleep in her room at night (which his puddling habit made impossible), and we were never able to make it clear to him that he must *not* scratch at her door after she had gone to bed.

Anne was the little sister, who would swoop down on him, whirl him up for a quick hug, then ease him to the floor again and go racing off. He would never have tolerated such exuberance from any of the rest of us, but he was always ready to romp with Anne. Her closet was his favorite playground and he kept his best treasures under her bed. He liked to nap there too, taking refuge in the darkest corner whenever the outside world became too overwhelming.

As for me, I was clearly the mother figure (nineteenth-century materfamilias style), the one member of the family who really belonged to him. I alone could always be interrupted, ordered about, imposed upon, depended on. He spent as much time as possible lying between my feet as I worked at my desk or in the kitchen. If I had to move about, he would sigh heavily, get up, and come toiling after me, only to plop himself down again as soon as I paused for even a second. When he was alarmed, he came skittering to me for protection. When he was lonely, he tugged at my skirt demanding to be picked up. When he was feeling irritable, I was always the first person he tried to bite.

Such individualized responses must reflect at least a degree of intelligence.

Secret was also able to modify his own innate behavior patterns in certain instances so as to adapt to the human world. Not that he put himself to any trouble in order to please us, but he did seem to have figured out at least one important point about human beings—that they depend on their eyesight more than skunks do. Surely a wild skunk in the forest, trundling along at midnight, seldom has occasion to look *up*. In fact, it is probable that he rarely lifts his nose from the ground. Yet Secret was continually craning back his head, trying to look us in the eye. We worried sometimes that all this unnatural effort would give him a stiff neck.

Another possible indication of intelligence is the fact that he reacted to the human voice. He recognized his own name and—usually—came when he was called. He could even pick his name out of the stream of speech.

One day Alice was explaining to Anne that she thought the best thing about valentines is that they are secret. Suddenly a cold nose touched her ankle, and there he was.

In addition to his name, Secret recognized the word "No!" In fact, he reacted to this particular word so strongly that if he overheard someone saying in an emphatic tone, "I'm sorry, but I simply don't KNOW!" he would go diving under the nearest bed, even though his conscience might have been perfectly clear.

Anne maintains that he also knew the word "Dinner," and this does seem likely.

A three-word vocabulary might not seem very impressive to anyone who has lived with a Siamese cat or trained an Irish setter to follow voice commands in the field. But both dogs and cats use some form of oral communication, not only with humans but also with their own kind. Skunks almost never do.

Secret had been with us for six months before we discovered that he could produce any sound at all. We simply assumed that skunks, like rabbits, are voiceless. Then one day he landed in the middle of a sirloin steak just as I was sliding it into the broiler. When I attempted to shake him off, he buried his teeth more deeply in the meat and growled. It was only a tiny gurgle, deep in his throat; I would not have heard it if I had not been so near. But it was unmistakably meant to be a growl. (It worked, too. The family had canned beef stew that night.)

On another occasion, Jim was trying to put him into the car and Secret, whose nap had been interrupted, was resisting with all the tenacity of one of the stubbornest creatures on earth. Somehow, Jim lost his hold for a moment and dropped his struggling armful onto the pavement, then with a wild lunge grabbed him up again. As he whooshed through the air, Secret let out a small, desperate squeal. Again, it was only a mouse-sized sound, but it was definitely a sound.

In addition to his so-called growl and his squeal of distress, Secret occasionally made a third kind of noise. We discovered it during a family get-together, when he encountered for the first time my mother's Abyssinian, Amber. At my mother's insistence, the kitten had been kept at a safe distance from Secret ever since we arrived (though whether for his protection or hers, I was not sure). Amber, of course, was burning with curiosity about the strange intruder. Inevitably the time came when she managed to slip into the living room when Secret was having his turn there.

He was contentedly sniffing under chairs, finding all sorts of lovely crumbs, and he paid no attention to the tiny, wild-eyed creature that began to creep up on him, tail lashing, fur ablaze, obviously planning to attack. As for us, we were frozen, unable to move, scarcely able to breathe.

Paw by paw Amber drew nearer until suddenly, quite by chance, Secret happened to veer toward her and they came face to face. The kitten stopped short, then bunched herself for a leap. Secret held perfectly still, seeming to evaluate the situation. Then, ever so slowly, he began to back away from her. Amber stared in fascinated surprise. Head down as if he did not see her, careful not to make an unexpected move, the skunk drifted further and further backward until he had reached what he judged to be the proper spot. Then he looked directly at the kitten and hissed. That hiss was the loudest, most effective sound in his entire repertoire. Amber shot into the air and flew to the top of the bookcase. Secret waited a moment, then calmly resumed his snack hunting.

So it would seem that skunks are quite capable of using oral communication if necessary. But as a rule, they don't bother, except during babyhood, when they sometimes have to chirrup to their mother for help. Considered against such a background of innate behavior, it seems remarkable that Secret paid any attention whatsoever when people were talking.

In spite of all this, we are still not sure how to answer when someone asks whether skunks can be considered intelligent.

As far as I know, scientific evidence is nonexistent. Researchers in laboratories seem to concentrate on rats and pigeons; naturalists in the wilderness study wolves and golden eagles. And then there are the chimpanzee trainers and the dolphin experts. But no one pays much attention to skunks. (Except to analyze their stomach contents!)

So for the time being, we evade the question on the grounds that we are not qualified to make a judgment, having known only a single skunk.

But what about that one skunk? I would not put Secret's intelligence anywhere near the level of a dog's or a cat's. (Or even a pig's, if recent research is correct!) He learned to tell the different members of the family apart. He played games, looked us in the eye, and knew his own name. He was good at tricking us into giving him forbidden snacks. He probably would have been a whiz at learning to poke a certain lever or follow a particular maze if there were plenty of bacon as a reward. But he never displayed any dazzling examples of problem-solving or complex reasoning.

Of course, a house skunk's environment is not very challenging. Who knows what intellectual capacities he might reveal in the woods, where he could be judged in terms of his proper world?

XII

AFTER WE ACQUIRED A PET SKUNK, people we had not seen in years began to drop in unexpectedly, accompanied by bevies of small sons and daughters, nieces and nephews, and assorted unidentified youngsters. It was amazing how many people just happened to be passing by.

Secret rather liked having visitors, provided that they arrived in late afternoon or early evening when he was feeling sociable. For one thing, he soon learned that visitors were invariably a good source of forbidden treats —chocolate cookies and cheese crackers and the like. Then too, I think he enjoyed being admired. If the younger guests became too rambunctious, he simply vanished under the couch for a bit. "Look there! You've scared the poor little fellow away!" someone was sure to say reprovingly. Calm would be restored instantly, and before long the poor little fellow would come inching out to rejoin the party.

Secret's visitors not only supplied him with unscheduled goodies and plenty of admiration, they also provided him, unknowingly, with entertainment. A house skunk's restricted human environment is, by and large, monotonously predictable. Floor lamps do not come crashing down on windy nights like oak boughs falling across a forest path. The rugs smell just about the same from day to day. It never even snows indoors. Being the lover of routine that he was, Secret probably didn't mind too much. But he was curious, and people-watching was one of the few interesting activities available to satisfy his curiosity. Even that did not amount to much in a family like ours where people spend so much time reading or listening to music or working at desks. So visitors were always a special treat.

Alice's friend Cathy Holton was one of the best. When she came to our house, there was never a dull moment for an observant skunk. Together she and Alice did all sorts of mystifying things.

The first time Secret saw Cathy she had come home with Alice from a ballet rehearsal. The two girls began spinning around the living room, practicing their pirouettes and piqué turns, when gradually they began to feel that they were being watched.

And so they were, from under the armchair.

When they finally collapsed breathless on the floor, their fascinated spectator crept slowly out and cautiously made his way over to them. He sniffed dubiously at their ankles, then peered worriedly into their faces. Clearly he was of the opinion that they had gone straight out of their minds, but he still couldn't resist investigating for himself.

After that first time, he never missed a practice session, doubtless the first skunk in history with a liking for ballet.

If human visitors became increasingly frequent at our house, animal visitors were rare. Someone occasionally brought a hamster or a guinea pig to call, but Secret never paid much attention. Perhaps he remembered his first discouraging experience when he was young.

Alice and Anne came back from a country walk one day with the exciting news that they had met three children biking down the road, one of whom had a young Dutch rabbit riding in her bicycle basket. What is more, the girls wanted to invite the rabbit for a visit that very afternoon.

"Seekie might like a playmate, you know," Anne said earnestly.

I hesitated. It ought to be all right. A skunk and a rabbit were not likely to hurt each other, especially when they were both so young. And it would be interesting to see how they got along. So I agreed, on condition that the visit be restricted to the Barbecue, the screened summerhouse beside the pond. I promised to provide refreshments all 'round: lemonade, fresh brownies, bacon scraps, and a raw carrot.

The rabbit arrived in a canvas beach bag, looking very alert and very self-confident. She was twice as large as Secret. Bunny, for this was her name, seemed delighted with the Barbecue. It was full of meadow smells, and she hopped about scenting the breeze and occasionally rising up on her hind legs to scan the surroundings.

Her host, meanwhile, was busy trying to dig a beetle out of a crack in the stone foundation and did not at first realize that she was there. Then suddenly, he caught a whiff of something strange. He whirled, flared, thumped. What was this enormous creature? It was not a human being, that was quite plain. It had black-and-white fur, much like his own. But whereas he was all tail and almost no ears, this stranger was just the opposite.

Bunny ignored him.

Secret thumped again; then, still getting no response, he scampered up to the astonished rabbit and pounced at her back. She bounded away as if she were a jack rabbit, and in two magnificent leaps had reached the far end of the Barbecue.

The little skunk stared about him in obvious puzzlement. Where had the thing disappeared to? Then, catching the scent once more, he set off pell-mell in pursuit.

The rabbit saw him coming and froze. Again Secret rushed up and again he pounced at Bunny's back. Was he perhaps remembering how he used to play with his brothers and sisters? Certainly his actions seemed playful rather than aggressive. The rabbit, however, did not want to play. Once more, she took off.

Secret paused as if to think things over, then shook himself and trotted back to his beetle hunt. For him, human visitors were much more rewarding.

One human visitor, however, was never welcome as far as Secret was concerned. This was a charming New York neighbor, with whom we often exchanged babysitting. (Or *sitting*, as our age-conscious daughters insist on calling it.) Our neighbor seemed very fond of animals and I'm sure never directed an unkind word at Secret. But nevertheless he did not like her.

Perhaps it was the way she talked—her voice was rapid and high-pitched; or perhaps it was the way she moved —nervously energetic and unpredictable. Whatever the reason, when she walked into the apartment, our skunk disappeared.

His presence was still felt, however. Soon after she arrived, a strong odor would begin to permeate the house. It was not the familiar stench, of course, for Secret had been descented. (Besides, even when very angry, he never attempted to spray, though as a baby he sometimes made a mock feint as part of a game; like all young skunks, he seemed to enjoy bluffing.) But it was undeniably a *skunk* smell and it was very strong. If she stayed more than a few minutes, the effect was quite overpowering.

The reaction developed at their very first meeting. Unfortunately we ourselves were not present. It was December and Jim and I had tickets to a Christmas concert. The neighbor had offered to "sit" for us. When we left, she was embroidering, the girls were reading in bed, and Secret was asleep in the study. When we came home, the apartment was an igloo. Every window was open and the snow was blowing in over the sills. Secret was nowhere to be seen, but our unfortunate sitter was huddled in front of the television, swathed in blankets.

"The children went to bed very nicely," she said, getting to her feet rather stiffly. "They're wearing sweaters under their bathrobes. And I met your skunk—he's perfectly enchanting. But, you know—well, I'm sure a skunk is a marvelous pet—so *unique* and all that—doesn't bark or scratch the furniture, either—but isn't it rather difficult adjusting to his scent?"

We sniffed. In spite of the arctic gales, the living room smelled like a zoo.

This had never happened before, but I realized that it would be the height of tactlessness to say so.

"Well," I said faintly, "it sort of comes and goes."

XIII

THE NEIGHBOR'S STRANGE EFFECT on Secret—and vice versa—was our first experience with a skunk's ability to produce what can only be called an *emotive* smell. The term is awkward, but it does describe a very curious phenomenon, which we did not notice when he was young but which became pronounced after he matured.

"Seekie must be angry," Anne would say, giving a practiced sniff as she passed the pantry, Secret's own private room. Very true: he had been ignored too much that day.

"What's been happening in my study?" Jim would ask, coming home from a late meeting. "Was the skunk shut in there accidentally?" Sorry to say, he was.

"Secret has to go to the vet today," I would tell the girls. "So remember to put on something old. You don't want to get your new sweaters all smelly." It was an important reminder, for as we sat in the waiting room holding him in our arms, he would begin to exude an odor which was not only strong but also very clinging.

I cannot explain just how he did it. Neither do I know whether the reaction could be consciously controlled, like frowning, or whether it came automatically, like nervous perspiration. In any case, the fact remained that whenever Secret was upset about something, you could tell it even with your eyes closed. Oddly enough, this special odor was very much like the smell of skunk cabbage in a marsh in early spring. It did not at all resemble that other smell which people usually think of as the typical skunk smell.

But even when he is feeling perfectly calm, a house skunk's fur keeps a certain characteristic scent. You can usually follow your nose to all his favorite nesting places throughout the house, and anyone who holds a pet skunk for a few minutes, especially on a rainy day, will find traces of this scent on hands and lap. To me, it is a pleasant smell—warm and musky, reminiscent of summer woods and moss and the edge of a pond where the reeds grow.

Having a skunk in residence lends an unmistakable *aura* to a city apartment.

Deodorizing shampoos are available, of course, as well as all sorts of special sprays and dusting powders, but our own experience with them is limited. Jim experimented once with a pet shampoo when he decided to give Secret a bath, but the experiment was never repeated.

The washing itself proved to be fairly easy. Jim used our city bathtub (the girls and I might have objected to this but we had gone to Connecticut), which he almost half-filled with lukewarm water. Secret turned out to be an excellent swimmer, paddling rapidly back and forth. He was too absorbed in looking for the way out to even notice the shampooing, but he did seem to enjoy being rubbed dry.

Unfortunately, the soap removed the delicate oils which give a skunk's coat its luster and it was almost a week before his fur regained its silky sheen. As for the deodorizing effect, Secret's own woodsy smell was masked for a while by a strong smell of soap, but we preferred the original.

Luckily, further baths proved unnecessary, as he somehow managed to keep himself immaculate, in spite of his fondness for the dustiest corners at the back of closets and under beds. He never forgot the experience, though, and sometimes when one of the girls was in the tub, he would come to investigate. Heaving himself up to the rim, he would peer thoughtfully down at the water. But he showed no signs of wanting to repeat his swim, and if we led him down to our country pond, he would take one sniff at the water's edge and turn firmly away.

For a wild skunk, of course, the ability to produce a powerful odor—and with it, a burning spray—is all-important. Often his life may depend on it.

This unusual method of self-defense is the result of a highly specialized development of the anal glands. Dogs and many other animals have similar glands but none so well developed.

The skunk's two scent glands are embedded in muscle tissue on either side of the rectum. They produce an amber-colored fluid (whose main element, butyl mercaptan, was formerly used in making certain perfumes to add a clinging quality) which can be sprayed out through re-tractable ducts. The ends of these ducts shoot out through the sides of the anus and then retract again with lightning speed, thus preventing any of the fluid from getting on the skunk himself: it is the victim that reeks, not the skunk. (In the descending operation these two glands must be removed with great care so as not to damage the rectal wall. The task is especially difficult—for all concerned—because most veterinarians prefer not to use an anesthetic, as it is difficult to estimate the correct amount.)

The skunk may fire off one gland or both together in a powerful spray, and he can repeat the process again and again if necessary. His aim is good for ten feet or more; the odor has been known to carry at least half a mile. The fluid stings the skin and burns the eyes, sometimes causing temporary blindness. The smell alone makes most animals sick. What is more, it does not begin to fade until days later. An encounter with an angry skunk is not easily forgotten.

A variety of remedies have been suggested for treating a dose of skunk spray: multiple washings with tomato juice, ammonia, gasoline, bleach, and chloride of lime have all been recommended among other antidotes. Some of the treatments sound worse than the problem. Obviously, avoiding the experience altogether is the best course.

This is not difficult to do, since the average wild skunk is a thoroughly peace-loving citizen. He will put up with an unbelievable amount of harassment before he resorts to his principal weapon. When he does take a stand, however, nothing can make him budge. Indians on the warpath, aware of this trait, sometimes wore ankle bands of skunk fur as a sign that they too would never run from danger.

We once saw a wildlife film in which a full-grown (but obviously inexperienced) grizzly bear chased a skunk for a good twenty minutes—through the woods, across a meadow, into a wide stream, and up a steep embankment. From time to time the exasperated little skunk would whirl to face his tormentor, flare his tail, and stamp his familiar warning, but the huge bear paid no attention. It was only when the skunk was clearly exhausted that he finally came to a skidding stop, and this time he did not face his pursuer. A moment later the grizzly also came to a stop; then, swinging his head from side to side in distress, he went lumbering back toward the cooling water. The skunk waited a moment to be sure that the coast was really clear before he pottered off in search of crickets.

That particular bear must have led an unusually sheltered life. More typical is the reaction reported by a forest ranger who saw five large bears move hurriedly away from the dump where they were feeding when one small skunk happened along.

The wild skunk's attitude of "You go your way, I'll go mine" extends to chance encounters with human beings as well. This we know from personal experience.

The first time we took Secret to Cape Cod, we established him in the cellar of my mother's house, which is cut into the hillside with a sandy terrace outside the cellar door. Going down to give Secret his supper late that first night, Jim thought he saw something moving across the terrace. It was a moonless night, but even so the stripe was clearly visible.

"Secret!" Jim said. "How in the world did you manage

to get out?" He bent over and found himself about to pick up, not our fragile baby, but a handsome, full-grown wild skunk, which was looking up at him in mild surprise.

"Sorry, old fellow," Jim muttered hastily.

The skunk seemed perfectly calm. He watched with interest as Jim backed slowly off, step by step. And he was still waiting when Jim returned with the rest of us, all holding our breath but eager to see the visitor.

Alice and Anne brought with them a dish of cat food, which they gently set down on the sand next to the bayberry bushes. It took the wild skunk about three gulps to finish off the meal. We watched, fascinated. Anyone might think that we had never seen a skunk eat before.

When he was done, the new skunk raised his head and looked over at us expectantly. Once he realized that we were not going to produce any more food, he picked up the dish by the rim and disappeared with it down the embankment, heading toward the beach. A collector, apparently.

The following night he was back for more cat food and another dish.

My mother named him Blackberry and has been feeding him ever since. Sometimes if she is late in setting out his meal, she finds him waiting on the doorstep. People coming to call on her are naturally disconcerted, and she often discovers a visitor marooned in the car, signaling wildly through the windshield. But in two years the only real problem has been to find a dish too heavy for Blackberry to carry away.

XIV

We had originally expected that our pet skunk would take more of a part in our daily activities—going for polite walks on his leash, dropping in on the neighbors, causing a sensation at the supermarket. But his seemingly uncontrollable habit of leaving a trail of puddles wherever he went inevitably cut down on excursions away from home—except for school visits.

As news of his presence spread through our city neighborhood, invitations from schools multiplied. We accepted as many as possible. I felt that it was good for him to meet a variety of people (skunks easily become one-family or even one-person pets), and I hoped that it was good for children to find out what this reputedly fearsome animal is really like.

For some reason, on such occasions he conducted himself like a perfect gentleman, never having accidents and never protesting the storm of excited pats and squeals. In fact, his behavior was better than at home. He stayed patiently on my lap or on a desk, and if set down on the floor, went bustling along the classroom walls, sniffing busily, either out of curiosity or, more likely, in a search for the way home. Before leaving, I would always pick him up so that every person could have a turn patting his soft fur, and he tolerated all the attention without ever snapping or hissing. He rather seemed to enjoy being in the limelight.

But if a classroom visit was a dramatic experience for Secret, transporting him to and from school was even more dramatic for his owner. I found—after trying a harness, a carrying case, and a grocery carton—that simply lugging him in my arms worked best. I would leave my coat unbuttoned and tuck inside as much of him as I could manage, which because of his size was not much. And his rear and tail would usually dangle over my arm. I hoped that if I kept at least his head under cover, he would be reassured by the darkness. Nevertheless, from time to time he insisted on peeking out in shocked disbelief at the city scene.

It was surprising how few human passers-by ever noticed me as I walked along a New York City street carrying a skunk. Their dogs noticed, though.

Nose to pavement, they would come trotting along, well-mannered and urbane, until they got within scenting range. Then they would stop short, eyes staring, hackles rising, nose fixed.

"Bismarck, *come!*" the owner would say, jerking on the leash. But Bismarck would not come. Slowly, cautiously, as if creeping up on a snake, he would be edging closer and closer to the source of that unbelievable smell.

"I'm terribly sorry," the owner would usually apologize, still not really looking at me. "I can't imagine why he insists on following you. He's never acted like this before!"

Even when I wasn't carrying Secret, walking in the city took on new drama. My shoes seemed to be thoroughly impregnated with the odor of skunk, although I myself couldn't notice it. As a result, I moved down Broadway like some sort of unintentional Pied Piper.

The most memorable occasion was the day I passed our local flower shop when their resident Dalmatian happened to be snoozing in the open doorway. She awoke instantly, made a dash for my feet, took one incredulous sniff, then flung herself down on her haunches, nose to the sky, and began to howl. Obviously she had learned a thing or two about skunks at some point in her life. I hurried along, trying to appear unconcerned. Two blocks later I looked back. The bewildered owner was kneeling on the sidewalk, vainly trying to console his dog, but she was still howling piteously. After that, I made a point of detouring around that particular shop.

Jim's shoes were somewhat less enticing, probably because Secret slept on them less often. However, Jim too had his share of embarrassing moments, usually involving a little old lady's Chihuahua or Pekingese. He kept hoping for some fashion model's Afghan.

Alice and Anne quickly came to enjoy this unexpected side effect of owning a skunk and loved nothing more than taking a stroll across the nearby Columbia University campus amid a flock of mystified huskies, dachshunds, collies, and spaniels. Sneakers, the girls soon found, worked better than loafers, but any shoes at all from our house proved to have a magical effect.

City walks would be even more dramatic, of course, if a skunk were actually ambling at your heels. Alice and Anne never gave up the hope of leash-training Secret. They loved the thought of being able to walk casually down the street while he went nosing along behind them. (Though I shudder to think how New York dogs would react to *that*.)

And in Connecticut, they planned to take Secret on exploring trips far outside the yard, if only he would submit to going on a leash.

When he was small, he followed us around the house so closely that it was hard not to step on him. Single file, nose-to-tail, is the typical walking style of a skunk family. In such a procession, even the most nearsighted baby does not get lost. It seemed to us that it should be easy to combine this inborn trait with the use of a leash. It did not work out that way, needless to say.

We bought an elegant scarlet cat harness with matching leash, which he liked so much that he often took it to bed with him. The problem was that he liked to play with it—not to wear it. (I don't know how wild skunks react to a snake, but watching Secret kill his leash over and over again made me suspect that snake meat must be a prime delicacy for them.)

Probably we did not start the training early enough. At any rate, although he submitted to having the girls buckle him into his outfit, he utterly refused, as Anne put it, "to walk according to the leash." On the contrary, he would yank with all his might in the opposite direction. Full-grown, he was strong enough to drag both girls with him.

The only successful method of taking him for a walk

was to leave him completely free and to control his wanderings by luring him with tidbits. The method was too hazardous for New York but worked well in Connecticut.

The girls were not easily discouraged from leash training, however, and from time to time, especially in the country, they would wrestle him into his harness and attempt a civilized stroll. Once the last loop had been fastened he simply ignored the whole thing: he was too enraptured by all the outdoor sounds and smells to pay attention to leather straps or human companions. Besides, whenever he went ducking under a rosebush in pursuit of an enormous grasshopper, it was quite clear who was really in charge.

XV

WILD SKUNKS ARE NOT SOCIAL ANIMALS. Except during the mating season or when caring for a newborn litter, both males and females prefer a solitary life. In winter several skunks may share the same den for warmth, but typically they go their separate ways with the first spring thaw.

Our house skunk clearly relished companionship—as long as he could enjoy it on his own terms. Growing up in the wilds, he would not have known this satisfaction. If Secret had been born in the woods, he would have left his mother and forgotten his littermates after a few months. There would have been nobody to play games with him. Or rub his tummy. Or keep him company during a windstorm.

Nevertheless, early last June he did sample the solitary life of a wild skunk. The girls and I were spending a brief week end in Connecticut, and Secret had come with us. We could stay for only one night. Alice was dancing the next week at Lincoln Center in the New York City Ballet's production of *A Midsummer Night's Dream*—presumably as one of Oberon's butterflies, although her costume looked more like a hornet. Anne was scheduled to play *two* recorder solos—a Bach gigue on the soprano recorder and a Mozart "aire" on the alto—for the annual music assembly at school. Last, and certainly least, I myself had a conference on Monday evening.

So it had to be a quick trip. But we wanted to catch the last of the apple blossoms, and we thought that Secret needed to get some fresh air. As it turned out, he got more than we had planned.

He was glad to be back in the country house and while the girls and I were fixing supper, he went off to explore his old trails and revisit his favorite hiding places.

It was not until we sat down to our steaks and nobody turned up to demand a share that we wondered where he might be.

"He's probably celebrating by taking a nap somewhere," I said. "He'll be out as soon as he smells steak."

But supper ended and the dishes were done and still no skunk. By now we were all apprehensive. I handed out flashlights and steak scraps, and we spread throughout the house, looking in every conceivable spot.

We did not find our skunk. What we did find was an unlatched screen door, slightly ajar.

Out into the dark yard we went, calling his name and waving steak. Every now and then we paused to listen for the telltale sniffing and rustling that always marked his progress outdoors. Nothing.

We searched every bush and every clump of tall grass in the entire yard, then circled down to the pond and across to the hill.

Finally I sent Alice and Anne upstairs to put on their pajamas while I took the car and cruised slowly along the road, watching the underbrush for the slightest movement and calling as I went. Still nothing.

The search had to be discontinued for the night. We left the back-kitchen door propped open and a banquet of steak in his dish. Then we went to bed and tried very hard to sleep.

The next morning the dish was untouched and it was plain that only mosquitoes had used the open door. We knew that it was useless to hunt for him during the day, since he would be denned up somewhere sleeping (and after such an adventure-filled night he would probably be sleeping extra hard), so we spent the morning driving to all the nearby farmhouses, explaining the situation to the neighbors.

"Good thing you warned us," people said, time and again. "Otherwise he'd have been shot on sight. We don't allow skunks fooling around our place."

We were scheduled to return to the city that same afternoon. But how could we go off without our skunk?

"Look," Jim said when I telephoned him for a frantic consultation. "You bring the girls in as planned. There's nothing more you can do anyway as long as it's daylight. Then I'll take the car and come out myself for the night. With any luck, I'll get there just about sunset, which will be exactly right."

So that is what we did. All through the week, in fact,

somebody drove out from New York every night. After a while we abandoned any further active hunting, but we always kept Secret's favorite door open and his supper waiting. The one time when the whole family had to be in the city—it was Alice's opening night—a teen-age neighbor, Erwin, took over the vigil. Erwin had often helped out with odd jobs about the house and he was one of the few people, apart from the immediate family, whom Secret might recognize. Secret, however, did not appear.

It was a long week. A week of uninterrupted breakfasts and quiet evenings, in a house where the garbage pail could stand unguarded and dropped slippers remained where they fell. Nobody scattered Anne's doll picnic or left a puddle beside Alice's desk. Nobody made off with Jim's best eraser or nagged me at bedtime. If a June bug blundered through the window, it was only a nuisance, not a prize.

When the week end finally came, we made the trip to Connecticut in record time. There was still no sign of our missing house pet, and a canvass of the neighbors failed to produce any news.

"My German shepherds did raise a ruckus here the other morning, about five o'clock," one man told us, "so I let them out. But when they came back they weren't blooded, so I guess they didn't find anything."

"It's been over a week now," Jim said gently to the girls that night. Unlike me, he believes in facing facts. "I'm afraid Secret's gone for good."

It was unseasonably cold and rainy, and Jim had

built us a veritable Yule blaze on the old hearth. Alice and Anne were toasting marshmallows but they didn't seem to be eating many.

There was a sudden rap at the back door. It was Erwin.

"Got some news I thought might interest you folks," he said casually. "There's a skunk moseying along Jeremy Swamp Road and he looks awfully fat to be a wild one."

"I think maybe you ought to go by yourself," Jim said to me.

Alice ran to get me some Cheddar cheese and Anne flew to straighten Secret's nest in the broom closet and refill his water dish. Jim backed the car around and turned it in the right direction: he probably didn't trust me not to head into the pond.

I tried to drive slowly, fearing that oncoming headlights on a rainy night might be enough to frighten whoever it was off into the woods. It seemed a long way.

At last, about half a mile down the road, I saw it—an unmistakable streak of silver moving slowly along in the darkness. No doubt about it—it was a skunk.

But was it our skunk?

I drew up some distance away and, leaving the headlights on, I softly got out of the car and began walking toward him.

"Secret!" I called. "Seekie! Is that you?"

The portly little shadow came to an abrupt halt.

Needless to say, I did the same. But now in the light from the car I could see him more clearly: the size, the marking, the face—it had to be Secret.

I took a step nearer, knelt down, and held out some cheese.

"Secret, don't you remember me?"

He turned away as if to go, then hesitated and looked back over his shoulder.

"Here, Secret! I've got some cheese for you. Wouldn't you like to come home?"

Again he hesitated.

Then, as if having reached a decision, he came toward me. He was, I noticed, limping quite badly.

I gave him the cheese and rubbed him behind the ears. Finally, when he made no further move to go, I lifted him gently into the car. All the way home he insisted on lying across my feet, which made driving rather precarious but no matter.

I carried him in my arms across his familiar yard and into the back kitchen where the welcoming committee waited. He twisted loose and slid to the floor. At once he began to go from person to person, sniffing at shoes and making sure who was who.

"Let's sit on the floor very quietly," Anne said, "and give him time to get used to us again."

Hobbling as if he had strained a shoulder muscle, Secret next moved to his water dish. He drank five bowls without stopping. Then he accepted some chicken, but he seemed less interested in food. His sides were bulging—a wilderness diet had certainly been agreeing with him. (Or had he perhaps been helping himself to the food some farm wife set out for her barn cats?)

Aside from the limp, he did not seem any the worse for wear. His fur was, as always, immaculate—not a burr, not a tick anywhere. And he was scarcely damp, although it had rained hard earlier in the evening: his outer coat was slightly misted but the thick inner fur next to the skin was completely dry. He did have a totally new smell, however, rather like one of those balsam pillows— Souvenir of Beautiful Bar Harbor—which would not be surprising except that we do not have balsam trees in this region.

He accepted hugs from each girl in turn and a friendly, man-to-man pat from Jim. Last of all he turned to me and flung himself on the floor in his favorite position between my feet. He gave a single sigh and went instantly to sleep.

"Do you think he's back for good, Mom?" Alice asked. "Or is he going to try again as soon as he's rested?"

"I have no idea," I said. "But let's hope he doesn't. Another time, you know, it might not turn out so well."

Much later, Jim and I were sitting in front of the fire, watching the last of the embers wink out.

"I keep wondering about one thing," I said. "It occurs to me that if I'd been looking for a lost puppy, I wouldn't have felt the need to take any snacks with me. Do you think Secret came to me because he really wanted to—or just because of the cheese?"

"I guess we'll never know," Jim said. "But we do know one thing. For whatever it's worth: when you found him coming down Jeremy Swamp Road, he was at least heading in the right direction. He was heading toward home."

XVI

AFTER SECRET CAME BACK from his week as a wild skunk, one question kept bothering me: Just how did he feel about us? Did he regard us merely as good providers— or as friends? Is it possible for a wild animal such as a skunk to feel any affection for a human being? For that matter, is the reverse possible either? (Of course I have read about those lions and otters who have lived so closely with people, but I know of them only second-hand. Persons like our friend Ann Mayer, who has a magic touch with injured birds, and the hermits who live in the north woods with bear cubs, fawns, bobcats, and assorted chipmunks and chickadees obviously have a special rapport with nature that most of us do not possess.)

Earlier, I would have said that the exact quality of our relationship with Secret was too ambiguous to define. But now I was not so sure.

During the week that he was gone, we discovered,

rather to our surprise, that we missed him. In spite of all the ups and downs we had been through with him, a genuine attachment had developed. We had become very fond of our funny, stubborn little housemate. He had added an extra dimension to our family life, and once we gave up trying to make him conform to human patterns, we learned to enjoy living so close to forest ways and habits.

I am less certain about Secret's own feelings. Obviously, he appreciated us as his main source of food—although I worried about the idleness that resulted. In the woods he would have needed to spend every waking moment in the search for food. In our household, where meals arrived, so to speak, on a silver platter—or at least on a plastic puppy dish—one of the major activities of a skunk's life became unnecessary. I often thought that I should scatter Secret's supper in little bits all around the house so that he would have to hunt for it, but I never carried out this benevolent project.

We also provided him with the sort of orderly existence a skunk likes, and if domestic life is rather monotonous with its unchanging pathways and unvarying weather, it is also comfortable and safe, values which no skunk in his right mind would underestimate.

Then too, whenever he was in the mood for a romp or wanted to have his chin scratched, he could usually find some human who would oblige. And if anything went wrong, he could depend on being rescued promptly.

In fact, as far as Secret was concerned, we were always on call. One week end, for example, we were in Connecticut. It was midafternoon and I was working at my desk. Secret was presumably asleep in the broom closet. And yet I had an odd feeling that he was awake.

I am not given to psychic intuitions, but from time to time I do get a feeling about something. Never about anything useful, such as the winning number in a game or the outcome of an election or the whereabouts of my missing wrist watch, but a vague little whispering at the corner of my mind that tells me whether the mail has come yet or who is on the telephone.

Once this feeling woke me from a sound sleep in the middle of the night and I sat up in bed, feeling certain that someone had called me. "What's the matter?" Jim asked groggily. Suddenly I knew the answer. "The African violets are cold," I told him as I reached for my bathrobe. They certainly were: the living-room window had been left open and the nearby plant table was getting the full blast of an icy wind. Of course this may not have been an example of a "feeling"—perhaps the violets had sent an SOS of their own.

At any rate, I do sometimes experience fleeting peripheral signals, and as I sat at my desk, I was absolutely sure that Secret was not where he should have been, curled up in his nest. I was equally certain that he was in trouble. What's more, I had a pretty good notion of where to find him. I didn't even need to leave my desk.

"Girls!" I called. "Check the stairs, will you? I think Secret's been trying to get up to the second floor again."

And indeed, there he was, stuck on the fourth step.

He was not allowed upstairs (because of possible lapses in house-training) and he knew it, but every so often, when no one was around, he felt impelled to try sneaking up there anyway. By now he had almost reached his full adult weight of twelve pounds, and it must take enormous effort for such a fat skunk to lift himself from one tall step to another. He never managed more than the first three or four before he had to give up. And it surely required courage to go even that high: skunks are not climbers. Yet again and again we found him on the stairs, stranded helplessly on the edge of a step, unable to go either up or down. (It was a miracle that he didn't fall backward and break a leg.)

He always seemed relieved but not surprised when help came. In this case, he gave each girl a sniff, yawned, and headed back toward the broom closet.

Food, comfort, security—life as a house skunk clearly has advantages.

Nevertheless, we would not have been surprised to have Secret turn against us when he became full-grown. So many wild animals make appealing pets when they are small but then "revert" as they approach adulthood. Only yesterday I met someone whose raccoon, the gentlest of house pets since infancy, had just been banished to a back-yard pen as a result of having bitten his owner on the cheek, torn an ear off the family spaniel (a long-time companion), and chased the teen-age son to the top of the dining-room table.

But although Secret became bossier and more impatient after his first year, he did not change much otherwise. To be sure, the brief mating season was marked by ill temper and a sudden interest in Anne's black snow boots. (Some veterinarians recommend castrating male skunks when they become sexually mature, at about five months, but our doctor does not advise it unless the skunk shows signs of turning vicious).

Also, during the winter's semihibernation, Secret became as grumpy as anyone might be who was disturbed out of a deep sleep. Aside from that, as Anne remarked on his first birthday, "He's the same as he always was, only more so."

But appreciating humans as providers of the good life and tolerating them as fellow residents of skunk territory is not the same as feeling affection for them as friends. For a long time, I was not sure that the term "affection" could even be applied in the case of a skunk—though I did hear stories which seemed to indicate that some skunks at least were capable of feeling a fondness for their owners.

Once at a P.T.A. affair I met a girl who told me a very unusual tale about her own house skunk. It seems that while she was in the hospital having her first baby, her pet skunk, Cyrano, stopped eating. When she came home, he refused to acknowledge her presence. It took her two days to make peace.

Then for a while, all went well. The baby slept in a bassinet in the living room; the skunk as always had his own basket in the study. Their schedules were different and they rarely saw each other.

The time came, though, when the baby outgrew the bassinet and the skunk's study had to be transformed into a nursery, complete with crib, playpen, freshly painted walls and the rest. Knowing how skunks dislike change, the parents were careful to leave Cyrano's basket in its usual corner. He would not have to give up his room entirely; he would only have to share it with a little roommate.

But as it turned out, he also had to share part of the mother's attention during his own active period, as the baby's teething problems began to require more and more nighttime rocking, singing, and so on.

Apparently, it was more than poor Cyrano could bear. Again he stopped eating, and this time he refused to be comforted.

"And so," the girl told me, "he died! Died of a broken heart!"

It is possible, of course, that Cyrano came across some cockroach poison somewhere. On the other hand, perhaps he really did die of jealousy. I cannot imagine Secret's doing anything so romantic.

But if high tragedy was not in Secret's line, he nevertheless did, on one occasion, give a clear demonstration of love. Or so it seems to me now.

It happened on a warm Sunday afternoon in New York. Jim and I had driven to Connecticut for the day to check on the furnace, leaving Alice and Anne in the city with the skunk. The girls were to finish lunch, clean up the kitchen, and then go next door to spend the afternoon with a seven-year-old neighbor, Andrea Lowman. Secret was asleep under the living-room couch and would probably not awaken, we thought, until we returned at suppertime.

The girls finished their chores as planned and then went over to Andi's, where they all settled on the floor with a pile of games. An hour or so later, Mrs. Lowman heard an odd clicking sound coming down her long hall. To her utter astonishment it was Secret, nosing his way toward Andrea's room, his long claws slipping on the polished floor.

Later we reconstructed his trail. He had apparently wakened at an unusually early hour and had first tipped over the garbage pail to make a meal of the lunch remainders, after which, feeling lonely, he went in search of the family.

The apartment was deserted. But then he passed the tall French windows, standing open to the breeze, and caught a well-known scent coming from the Lowmans' windows. Between the window sill and empty air was a narrow ledge, fenced with iron grillwork at its outer edge. The Lowmans' windows were separated from ours by an unfenced portion of the ledge. Secret must have ventured out on this ledge, twelve stories up, and somehow squeezed his way along to the neighboring sill.

Here he must surely have hesitated before entering a strange apartment, but he wanted to find his girls. So he clambered into the Lowmans' living room, paused long enough to dig up their prized potted rubber plant in search of worms and leave a small puddle on the new white rug, then headed unerringly for Alice and Anne.

A moment later a cautious black nose was poking around Andi's door, and then a happy skunk settled himself like a well-stuffed pillow right in the middle of the girls' checkerboard.

Of course they offered him a snack as a reward for bravery. He had, after all, risked his life.

"But you know," Andi's mother reported wonderingly, "I don't think he was after food, really. I think he just wanted to be with the girls."

And if this is not a sign of love, I don't know what is.

XVII

THE STORY SHOULD END HERE. When I began, this past summer, to put together the notes I had been keeping on our experiences with a house skunk—hoping to make a book of them—I expected to end at this point. But Secret provided his own ending. And it was not at all what I would have chosen.

One hot evening toward the end of August, Secret again let himself out of the house. He had shown no disposition to wander since his earlier adventure. But this was the height of the caterpillar season, and the entice-ments of the darkness outside must have been irresistible.

He may very well have had in mind only a brief walk around the yard. Perhaps he strayed further than he intended. In any case, when we finally missed him and went to search, there was no trace.

An hour later we heard the first rumble of thunder. The yard flashed silver and then the torrents began. Any hopes that Secret might find his way home by retracing his own trail were washed away in the downpour.

The next morning was clear—very hot and muggy—but that night another drenching rain fell. The pond overflowed its banks, and the following day the girls waded up to their knees inside the Barbecue.

Each day for the next six days, the daytime weather was clear but very hot, much too hot for a skunk to stir abroad; and every night for the next six nights, it rained. Hard.

We spent our days, as we had done once before, searching for news of our lost pet. We questioned all the neighbors but without results. This time, however, many of them were sympathetic. They had seen Secret taking his evening strolls with Alice and Anne and they could imagine how the girls must feel.

We took countless walks through the woods and countless drives along all the country roads, calling in vain. We posted signs in the local market, as well as in the post office, and put an ad in the weekly newspaper:

TAME SKUNK LOST!

Vicinity Jeremy Swamp Road.
Descented housepet named Secret.
If he turns up in your yard,
please give him bacon or cheese
and call 260-0000. Reward.

We received many replies. There was no doubt but that everyone for miles around heard about Secret and knew that he was missing. Since we had no idea how far a wandering skunk might range, we followed up every lead, no matter how unlikely. The countryside seemed to be overrun with nocturnal animals, but in every instance the nighttime visitor turned out to be a raccoon, opossum, stray dog, or barn cat. There seemed to be very few skunks in our part of Connecticut, wild or tame.

At last, we had to give up. Even so, for the rest of the summer, no matter what the weather, the back-kitchen door stood hopefully ajar. Our last act before returning to New York in the fall was to make one final circuit, both on foot and by car.

All this was months ago. I have put away the red leash, together with the old glove, the remains of the Christmas pine cone, and all the other treasures.

The girls will get a puppy this spring. They are old enough now for the responsibility and have certainly proved their gentleness and patience. They will be overwhelmed by the outpouring of devotion, I know, and by a puppy's eagerness to adapt himself to their ways, rather than insisting on just the opposite.

Jim, whose best boyhood memories involve his retriever, will again have a dog at his side on hikes and fishing trips.

And I will have another young thing about the house. But on week ends when we go to the country, Jim still slows the car as we drive along Jeremy Swamp Road and Alice still wakes in the night, certain that she has heard a familiar impatient scratching at her door. I notice that Anne still walks softly when she comes in for breakfast.

Now that we have moved back to the city for the

winter, Erwin keeps the Connecticut lookout, and so do our nearest farm neighbors, the Lovdals. They have a screech owl living near their barn and once played host to a family of red foxes under the woodshed. They would welcome a visiting skunk.

"He may be getting along just fine," Oscar Lovdal says. "Instinct is a good teacher."

"And remember," his wife, Jean, adds, "your skunk did leave of his own free will. You really shouldn't feel too guilty."

My mother says the same thing.

As for me, I lie awake on stormy nights, wondering whether Secret can possibly be still alive. Has he managed to evade the night-roaming dogs? The farmers' shotguns? The traps? The Saturday night cars?

There will be more houses and more cars if the new ninety-four-lot development is approved along Jeremy Swamp. Slowly, inexorably, the woods and marshes are disappearing here as in so many other places. What will become of the creatures that are living there now, I wonder? Where will they go when the bulldozers arrive?

And if the town carries out its plan for an aerial spraying against gypsy moths next spring, will a city skunk know enough not to eat poisoned caterpillars? For that matter, will any of the small mammals know enough to survive?

Dangers that used to seem remote to us have suddenly taken on a terrible relevancy. For the first time I wish that we could vote in this town, that we had enough influence —knew enough people—to make a difference. Next summer when we come back here, we will have to do something constructive. There must be many local people who share this feeling and surely there will be some way of translating concern into action.

It is odd that one little skunk—who went his own way like a small Swiss burgher, intent only on his own personal affairs—could have awakened in us this passionate sense of involvement.

Now, in midwinter, I remember how Secret hated the cold. Even with his heavy coat, he stretched as close to the hearth or to the radiator as he could. If he is still alive, does he ever miss the warm bed he used to have? And his bacon and Cheddar cheese? And his family?

I tell myself that the woodlands near our house are ideally suited to a skunk: plenty of glacial boulders and outcroppings to create caves, a number of streams and small ponds—and, Heaven knows, plenty of insects. I remind myself, too, that it is very pleasant to have my evenings to myself again. Also not to have to do so much mopping. (Perhaps next year we will even have the floors done over.) Our lives are undeniably easier now that he is gone.

But the shadow of a fat little skunk is always with us. Even after all these months, the country house still seems a place of invisible trails and secret dens. And in the city we still catch, in unexpected corners, a smell of the outdoors.

Yesterday we drove up to Connecticut. There was still some snow left after the last blizzard, so Jim and Alice decided to go sledding. Anne and I took a walk in the woods.

At the base of a granite ledge we came upon a single

paw mark in a patch of snow. It was small but very distinct, with the clear marks of long claws, like miniature bear claws.

"Oh, do you *think—?*" Anne breathed, more a prayer than a question. Out of her pocket she pulled a small packet of Cheddar cheese. "I always carry some," she said, "just in case."

She made a neat circlet of orange crumbs in the snow around the pawprint.

Everything was very still among the pines and bare maples. He should certainly have heard us calling his name. Unless, of course, he happened to be sleeping very soundly. Or decided not to answer. Or was not there at all.

This morning the girls report that the cheese is gone. But of course, raccoons and opossums probably also like cheese. The pawprint is gone too, melted away, and there are no others.

BY WAY OF THANKS

In writing this book, I have had enthusiastic family support: from my husband (appearing here under the *nom de guerre* of "Jim"), who combined the sternest criticism with the warmest encouragement; from my mother, whose letters asking about skunks first got me started keeping notes; and especially from Alice and Anne, who not only made all sorts of valuable suggestions but also nobly pitched into household chores so that I could have extra time at the typewriter.